# CLAM SHACKS

# CLAM SHACKS

## The Ultimate Guide to New England's Most Fantastic Seafood Eateries

### The Best Clam Shacks from Connecticut to Maine!

## Mike Urban

CIDER MILL PRESS

BOOK PUBLISHERS

Kennebunkport, Maine

13-Digit ISBN: 978-1-60433-208-7
10-Digit ISBN: 1-60433-208-5

This book may be ordered by mail from the publisher. Please include $3.50 for postage and handling.
Please support your local bookseller first!

Books published by Cider Mill Press Book Publishers are available at special discounts for bulk purchases in the United States by corporations, institutions, and other organizations. For more information, please contact the publisher.

Cider Mill Press Book Publishers
"Where good books are ready for press"
12 Port Farm Road
Kennebunkport, Maine 04046

Visit us on the web!
www.cidermillpress.com

Design by www.PonderosaPineDesign.com, Vicky Vaughn Shea and Sommer Fernandes

Typography: Gill Sans, Miller, Stars 'n' Strips, Zapf Dingbats

Printed in China

1 2 3 4 5 6 7 8 9 0
First Edition

**To Ellen and the kids**

LONG ISLAND
SOUND SHACKS

NARRAGANSETT
BAY SHACKS

CAPE COD
SHACKS

NORTH SHORE AND
NEW HAMPSHIRE
SHACKS

SOUTHERN
MAINE SHACKS

MID-COAST
MAINE SHACKS

# CONTENTS

THE Clam Shack of Kennebunkport, Maine.

# INTRODUCTION

Ever since Lawrence "Chubby" Woodman fried up some clams outside his roadside grocery stand on Route 133 in Essex, Massachusetts, back in 1916, clam shacks have been a permanent fixture of the coastal New England landscape. These casual, fiercely independent, family-owned and -operated eateries help define the region's character and cuisine, and patronizing them year after year has become a time-honored tradition for legions of families and gatherings of friends.

This book contains detailed descriptions of more than fifty of the best and most unique clam shacks to be found in New England. You'll meet the owners, get a good look at the shacks and their environs, and learn about what it's like to eat there as well as some of the tastiest and most unique dishes that each one has to offer. You'll also get the background on how each clam shack came to be and how each has changed (or, in many cases, stubbornly stayed the same) over the years. Recipes are scattered throughout the book, all of them kindly donated by clam shack owners for your enjoyment at home.

So, if you enjoy a day at the beach followed by a plateful of deep-fried seafood or a cool, refreshing ice-cream treat, take this book along with you this summer, explore New England's lovely and varied coastal realms, and hit as many of these shacks as you can. Clam shacks in New England are as soothing to the soul as they are to the belly.

# WHAT IS A CLAM SHACK?

**W**hen you bring up clam shacks in a conversation, it usually elicits knowing smiles from listeners. Perhaps they have fond memories of going to clam shacks in the past to enjoy some fine seafood and to seek respite from the blazing sun and crowded beaches in summertime. Just as often, however, the subject of clam shacks prompts the question: "What exactly *is* a clam shack?"

Good question. There is no strict definition of what a clam shack is. The term means many things to many people. Some clam shacks are little more than super-casual, shingled huts by the beachside, whereas others are full-blown, cavernous restaurants with brass rails, ceramic tile floors, silk flowers, and soft, cushiony booths.

There are, however, a number of characteristics that make certain seaside eateries more shack-like than others. Let's call them "shack factors." The more shack factors a place has, the more of a clam shack it is.

For the purposes of this book, there are two major qualifiers that more or less define clam shacks, along with several other factors that

**ALL** clam shacks must have deep-fried seafood.

help enhance a clam shack's distinction in the crowded field of seafood eateries. Here are the two biggies that are must-haves for all bona fide clam shacks:

1. **Deep-fried seafood.** If it's a clam shack, it has to serve deep-fried seafood of some sort or another, and the more the better. This is one of the few absolutes in the world of clam shacks. There are many restaurants that serve excellent deep-fried delicacies from the sea, but what sets clam shacks apart from other seafood restaurants is the second major qualifier, which is:

2. **Dining "in the rough."** Part of the fun of eating at a clam shack is the informality of it all. This includes dining in the

**ORDERING** your food from a window or counter is a key component of what makes a clam shack a clam shack.

rough—where you stand in line, order your food and drink at a window or counter, wait for your number to be called, then, with food tray in hand, seek out a spot to dine at a table or booth or, better yet, outside at a picnic table.

Here are several other shack factors that help define the widely varied and wonderful world of clam shacks:

○ **Kitschy building design and décor.** As Supreme Court Justice Potter Stewart once said of pornography—he couldn't define it, but he said, "I know it when I see it"—so it often goes with clam shacks. That is, when you pull into the parking lot and behold the crazy, funky exterior of the building and the shabby/chic décor inside, you know you're at a clam shack, and no one can convince you otherwise. To completely mangle another quote: "If it looks like a clam shack and smells like a clam shack, it probably *is* a clam shack."

○ **Cash only.** Most clam shacks are cash-only operations. Few accept credit cards, and some take personal checks. Most cash-only shacks have ATMs on the premises for customer convenience, but at the vast majority of clam shacks up and down the New England seaboard, cash is king.

○ **Outdoor seating.** Dining outdoors is a big part of the clam shack experience, and the more outdoor seating a place has (especially picnic tables scattered around the grounds), the more shack-like it is.

○ **Seasonal operation.** Although a handful of clam shacks stay open year-round, the majority are seasonal operations, typically opening in April or May and closing in

**DINING** outdoors really enhances the clam shack experience.

September or October. Chances are, if it's seasonal and it serves seafood, it's a clam shack.

⊘ **BYO.** Most clam shacks don't serve alcohol, preferring instead to offer soda, lemonade, iced tea, bottled water, and in some cases smoothies. Many shacks, however, have a BYO policy, so you may bring your own brew or your favorite bottle of wine to enjoy with your meal. Be sure to check ahead to see what rules any given clam shack may have so as to avoid any misunderstandings or disappointments.

⊘ **Plastic silverware.** You will rarely, if ever, find a clam shack that provides anything but plastic utensils with meals. This is in keeping with the (gasp!) almost total disposability of everything that comes with clam shack fare, including plates and sometimes even the trays and boxes on which the meals are served. Many clam shacks are getting greener in their materials and practices, but they're still basically dine-'n'-toss operations.

⊘ **Burgers and dogs.** Not everything that's cooked up at clam shacks comes from the sea. Most shacks boast excellent grilled hamburgers and hot dogs, as well as a variety of sandwiches and wraps. And don't forget the all-important lobster roll, a mainstay of clam shacks everywhere. If it doesn't have a nice, meaty lobster roll, then it probably isn't a clam shack.

⊘ **Ice cream.** In an attempt to provide the complete summertime alfresco dining experience, virtually all clam shacks serve up ice cream in one form or another. Some offer only a handful of hard-packed ice-cream flavors, whereas others roll out dozens of flavors in both hard- and soft-serve varieties. Many clam shacks additionally do a lot of baking, and you'll find some excellent homemade pies, brownies, and other desserts to tempt you while you order up your main meal at the window or counter.

Hopefully these qualifiers and characteristics help explain what makes a clam shack a clam shack and how the establishments in this book were selected for inclusion. So, enough with all this chatter—let's hit the road and do some eating!

BLOUNT

Clam Shack

WARREN RI

The Best
CHOWDA & CLAMCAKE
In Narragansett

FRED'S SHANTY

FAMOUS SINCE 1972

Coca-Cola

THE CLAM CASTLE

SEA SWIRL

FRESH SEAFOOD
FAMOUS FOR CLAM

ARNOLD'S
Lobster & Clam Bar

F-250
XLT SUPER DUTY

IGGY'S

DOUGHBOYS &
CHOWDER HOUSE

Monahan's

Clam Shack by the Sea.

CHAMPLIN'S SEAFOOD

HOMEMADE ICE CREAM & YOGURT

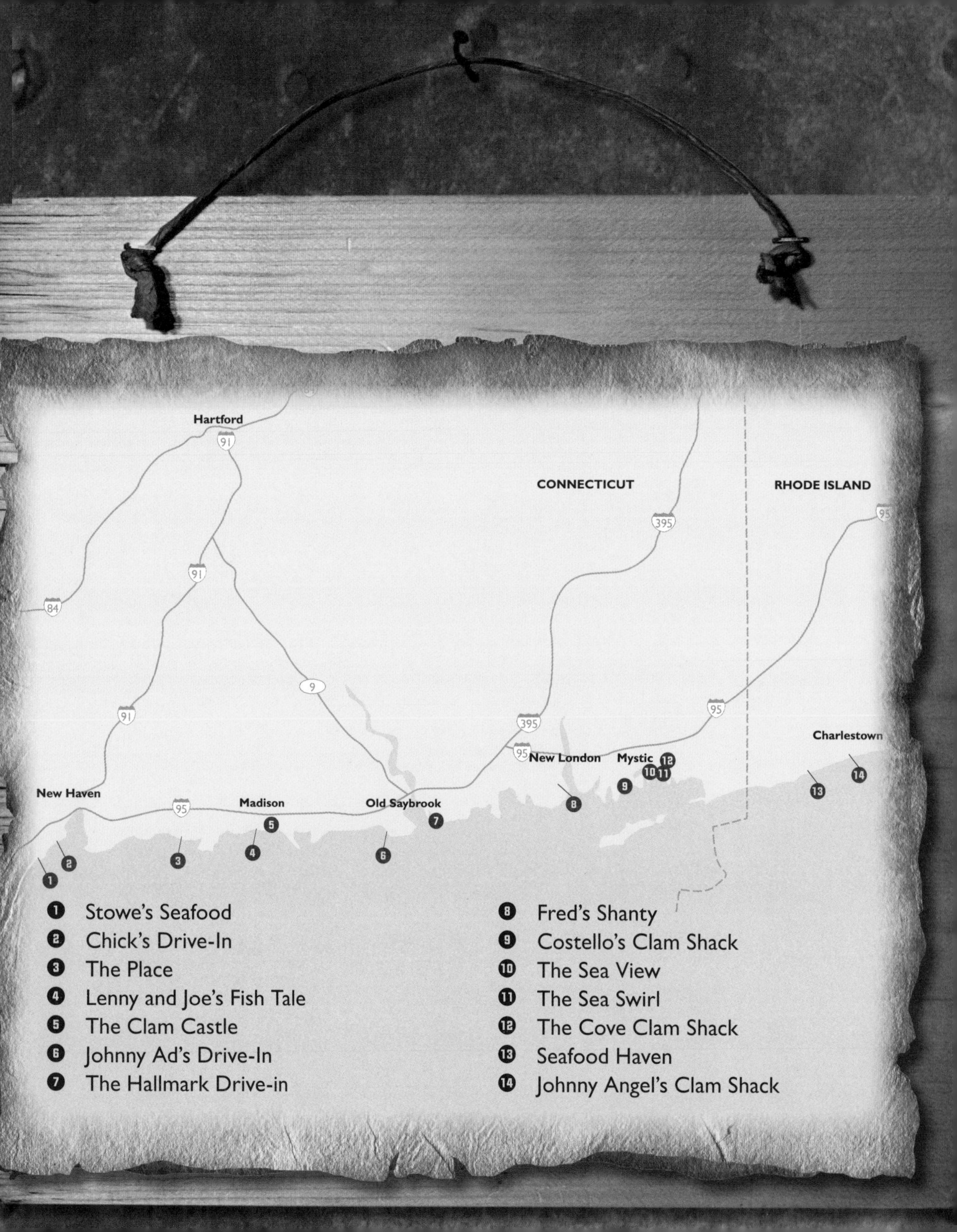

Hartford

91

CONNECTICUT

RHODE ISLAND

395

84

91

95

91

9

395

95

Charlestown

95 New London

Mystic 12

10 11

New Haven

9

Madison

Old Saybrook

Fred's Shanty 8

13

14

95

5

4

7

3

2

6

1

1 Stowe's Seafood

2 Chick's Drive-In

3 The Place

4 Lenny and Joe's Fish Tale

5 The Clam Castle

6 Johnny Ad's Drive-In

7 The Hallmark Drive-in

8 Fred's Shanty

9 Costello's Clam Shack

10 The Sea View

11 The Sea Swirl

12 The Cove Clam Shack

13 Seafood Haven

14 Johnny Angel's Clam Shack

# LONG ISLAND SOUND SHACKS

**F**or eons, Long Island Sound has been a bountiful fishery for all sorts of wonderful seafood—including clams! Even though very little commercial clamming is done in the area now, there are numerous clam shacks dotting the Connecticut shoreline and stretching into western Rhode Island, where fried clams, scallops, shrimp, and fish are served up to thousands of hungry customers every day, especially in the summer, and where more often than not, this bounty of the sea is enjoyed outdoors at picnic tables while dining "in the rough."

The clam shacks of Long Island Sound distinguish themselves in a variety of ways. Lobster rolls are often served warm, with the sweet lobster meat slathered in melted butter. The clear-broth type of clam chowder (often called Rhode Island style) is also prevalent here. And you'll find more flounder and sole on the menus than haddock and cod, as these flat-bodied, shallow-water bottom dwellers are locally plentiful.

U.S. Route 1 is the highway of choice for your clam shack journey along the northern shore of Long Island Sound. Many of the shacks are either on or within a mile or so of the fabled highway, and there are plenty of things to see and do as you make your way from one shack to the next.

So, what are we waiting for? Let's get started!

# Stowe's Seafood

347 Beach Street, West Haven, CT 06516 | (203) 934-1991 | Open year-round

**W**e begin our journey with this low-key clam shack nestled in front of a popular stretch of sand on Long Island Sound in the gritty, blue-collar city of West Haven, Connecticut. Stowe's is most likely the first bona fide clam shack that you'll encounter as you head north and east out of New York City into New England. This very

**STEP** right up and place your order at Stowe's friendly service counter.

casual eatery features stand-up ordering at the service counter, a cheery low-key atmosphere, lots of colorful locals, deep-fried and fresh seafood, loads of kitschy nautical décor, and a variety of outdoor seating options—all on a busy two-lane street that separates the restaurant from the beach across the way.

Co-owners Wayne and Karen Capone have run Stowe's from the same tree-shaded corner spot since 1980. It started as a fish market, selling fresh-off-the-boat delights to residents of the surrounding Italian-American neighborhood; chowders and deep-fried platters began appearing on the menu a few years later. Both businesses still thrive under the same roof. Wayne and Karen's first child was born shortly after Stowe's opened, and they went on to have a total of four children, all of whom have spent plenty of time over the years working in the family business.

Wayne grew up just a stone's throw from Stowe's current location, in a modest home behind Chick's Drive-In, West Haven's other famous shack. A self-described "rock rat," Wayne spent much of his youth clambering over

West Haven's then-rocky shoreline (the sand was trucked in later). Although his grandfather had been selling fish in various parts of West Haven since 1920, Wayne had no interest in getting into the business until he and Karen were married in the late 1970s and in need of a steady income.

**SEAFOOD** lovers will have a hard time ignoring this roadside sign in West Haven, Connecticut.

## KEEPING IT SIMPLE

Unlike many other successful clam shacks, Stowe's has stayed pretty much the same size since its opening some thirty years ago. The Capones have plans for a modest expansion in the next couple of years to increase indoor seating for their year-round customers, who constitute an important part of their business. But, unlike many of his competitors, Wayne prefers to keep his shack on the small side, and he still closes every night no later than 7 p.m. to give workers and Capone family members the opportunity to enjoy their evening hours.

When you first walk into Stowe's, it takes a couple of seconds for your eyes to adjust to the dim lighting—but it can be a soothing change on a glaringly bright summer day. Chalkboards above and behind the counter list the many menu options (seafood and otherwise). Friendly young folks in aprons take your order and hustle it to Wayne and the gang in the cramped, busy back-room kitchen.

Fish and chips are among the most popular and highly lauded dishes served up at Stowe's. Several Brits have raved that Stowe's fish and chips compares very favorably with the real thing back home. (See what truly fresh fish will do for you?) The Capones get their fillets from New Bedford, Massachusetts; Stonington, Connecticut; and other nearby commercial operations.

Hot chowder of the Rhode Island (clear broth) variety is a year-round favorite, especially on a cold winter's day. There are about ten different deep-fried seafood "boats" to choose from, including shrimp, haddock, sole, cod, scallops, clams, and oysters—all (except the shrimp) of local origin. Stowe's breads its seafood with unseasoned cracker meal for lightness and uses canola oil for frying. During the busy summer months, the oil is completely swapped out every two days max (frequently every day) to guarantee a light, crispy crunch.

The boats are served up on paper plates that are set in square-shaped, open-topped cardboard boxes, which help you to keep your highly stacked meal under control while feasting. The lobster rolls are served two ways: hot buttered (the preferred method of many clam shacks in southern New England) or in a cold salad mix containing celery and mayonnaise (the predominant method for rolls served from Cape Cod northward). The toasted buns are of the distinctive New England top-split variety.

One more menu item of distinction that deserves special mention: the seafood-stuffed clam, or "stuffie." This breaded snack contains a variety of minced shellfish (everything except clam meat, for some reason), mixed in a lightly seasoned stuffing and served warm in an oversized clam shell. Also, be sure to stop by in late spring and summer to sample the chewy, fresh soft-shell crabs from Maryland's Chesapeake Bay.

Once you've placed your order, you'll be given a white plastic square with your order number on it, sort of like the old-time bakeries. Don't wander too far away, though. When your order's ready, the counter staff will yell out your number two or three times (no PA system in these close quarters), so be sure to grab your food before somebody else does!

## Amusements Galore in the Days of Yore

The picturesque waterfront stretch in West Haven was once home to one of the largest amusement parks in the country. Savin Rock Amusement Park started attracting locals and tourists in the 1870s, and it continued to grow in size and popularity for the next 100 years. Roller coasters, games, rides, water slides, and lots of snack stands greeted people who initially arrived on foot, then by trolley, and eventually by car.

The Savin Rock shoreline underwent numerous transformations over the years as it grew and shrank, surviving and rebuilding after several hurricanes and tropical storms. Massive piers and boardwalks were constructed and constantly reworked to keep visitors coming back for more.

There's very little left of the old amusement park grounds, but you can relive those days of fun (in between clam shack visits!) by checking out the Savin Rock Museum at 355 Main Street in West Haven.

## AHOY, MATEYS!

Inside and out, this place has more than its fair share of nautical décor—lobster buoys, cork-ring life savers, fishing nets—everything you'd expect to see in a "themed" seafood restaurant, except that this stuff is the real deal. Wayne finds a lot of it on his occasional beachcombing strolls across the street. There are a few small tables inside, but you're usually better off finding a spot beneath the canopied row of picnic tables right outside the front door where you stand a much better chance of catching a cool sea breeze, especially satisfying on warm, sunny summer days.

There's a treasure trove of items relating to West Haven's colorful shoreline history scattered throughout the small indoor dining area. Wayne and Karen proudly display books, maps, and old photos of the waterfront, along with numerous items relating to pirates. (Definitely consider buying a Stowe's T-shirt, which prominently displays their famous logo: an eye-patched, bandanna'd skull sitting atop a couple of fish skeletons for crossbones.)

It's comforting to know that Wayne and Karen are generally content with their shack

**STOWE'S** shaded picnic tables provide a breezy break from the midday sun.

size and location and that their expansion plans are modest. Wayne claims that numerous regulars insist that he keep things the way they are, and he's happy to oblige.

A few things to keep in mind when gearing up for a visit to Stowe's: there are no restrooms on the premises, it's a cash-only establishment, and parking is limited. However, don't let these restrictions deter you from some of the best deep-fried seafood (and fresh fish) to be found in the metro New Haven area.

# Chick's Drive-In

183 Beach Street, West Haven, CT 06516 | (203) 934-4510 | chicksdrivein@yahoo.com | Open year-round

**T**alk about an institution! Chick's is where New England's deep-fried seafood tradition meets up with Connecticut's Italian-American blue collar community in a mega-shack that has been in the same location (and under the same ownership) for sixty years and that continues to cater to legions of loyal locals who come for the free beach parking and stay for the food.

This poured-concrete, deep-fried, drive-in empire is presided over by Vincent "Chick" Celentano, founder and potentate of fried clams and lobster rolls, West-Haven style. Chick got his start back around 1950 as a young man living on Beach Street, watching the traffic in front of his parents' home crawl to and from the (now defunct) Savin Rock Amusement Park a short distance to the west. He came up with the idea of selling hot food to this semi-captive audience, so he started cooking up burgers and hot dogs in the family's garage, eventually expanding into the deep-fried foods that have

**CHICK** Celentano, circa 1950s.

made Chick's famous. (The foot-long hot dogs remain a huge seller, along with the clams and lobster rolls.)

As business grew over the years, Chick eventually razed the family house and put up the current stand with its trademark open-air order counter facing the street in front, and he installed dozens of poured-concrete picnic tables outside that are mobbed by hundreds of hungry diners each day during peak season in July and August.

## Knock it Down, and They Will Come

The main draw to this breezy stretch of West Haven shoreline is the sandy strip of beach across the street from Chick's. In a stroke of marketing genius (and as a way to do something nice for the community), Chick began to buy up houses adjacent to the drive-in years ago (mostly beach shanties), raze them, and build an ever-expanding parking lot. He offered free, no-obligation parking for anyone wishing to go to the beach, and thousands have repaid his kindness over the years by patronizing his restaurant time and again. Chick takes pride in this symbiotic relationship. A sign over the main entrance reads, "Through These Doors Pass the World's Finest Customers." Chick placed it there early on, and it remains his credo to this day.

There are a few ways to enter Chick's, and if you come in from the front, you're face to face with a gleaming stainless steel counter and an enticing menu hanging overhead. Order at any of the three cash registers, pay up, then wait for your number to be called over the PA system. In good weather, the counter area has a very pleasant open-air feel to it, with breezes coming off the Sound and the occasional smell of salt spray in the air. Who's ready for some seafood?

**COME** for the free parking, stay for the food.

## What's Cookin' at Chick's

The most popular item at Chick's is the foot-long lobster roll, filled with buttery meat and piled high in a top-split bun. At $9.99, it's quite a bargain. Runner up are the fried whole-belly clams, which come out of the deep fryers sweet and crunchy/chewy; the platter version is stacked impossibly high with french fries and onion rings.

In recent years, Chick has reached out to his local following with a unique and very affordable "Recession Menu." In addition to the $9.99 lobster roll, you can get shrimp, scallops, calamari, clams, soft-shell crab, catfish, or oysters with side trimmings of crispy fries and creamy cole-slaw for the bargain basement price of $11.99. This is Chick's way of pulling in families who yearn for some deep-fried seafood but balk at the often high prices at many places.

When it comes to chowder, Chick's shows no regional favoritism. They've got it Rhode Island (broth) style, Manhattan (tomato-based) style, or creamy New England style—plus, there's a special Chick's version. All are chock-full of fresh clams and served by the cup or bowl.

After his sixty-some-odd years in the business, Chick says he owes his success to the simple formula that he calls "S + S = S"—sweat plus sacrifice equals success. Come to Chick's and see for yourself by enjoying some fine seafood on his patio next to Long Island Sound.

# The Place

901 Boston Post Road, Guilford, CT 06437 | (203) 453-9276 | theplaceguilford.com
Open late April to late October

Though The Place is not a clam shack per se (no deep-fried seafood and no order window or counter), this highly unusual eatery deserves special attention (and strong recommendation) for its unorthodox roadside setting, its fire-pit method of cooking, its amazing clams, and its all-around uniquely relaxed and enjoyable atmosphere. Where else can you dine outdoors on bright-red wooden tables festooned with fresh flowers, where tree stumps serve as chairs, where you can bring your own salads, side dishes, and libations, and where you can enjoy seafood, corn on the cob, steaks, and chicken, all fire-roasted over an

**THE** Place's owners, Vaughn (left) and Gary Knowles.

eighteen-foot-long, wood-fed fire pit? Only at The Place.

This one-of-a-kind roadside stand came into being in the 1940s, when an old salt named Whitey started a clam-bake stand on Route 1 in Guilford, Connecticut, about ten miles east of New Haven. He roasted clams over an open fire and served them to customers who dined alfresco at round, wooden-top tables while seated on tree stumps. In 1971, Vaughn Knowles, who had worked for Whitey as a teenager, purchased the stand and kept it going with its five-item menu of roasted clams, corn on the cob, shrimp, lobster, and steamers. Vaughn's brother Gary joined him shortly thereafter, and since then, the two brothers have been in business together for over forty years. During that time, The Place has grown into a regional dining phenomenon. A limited number of additional menu items, such as roasted fish, grilled steaks, and barbecue chicken, have been added over the years, but simplicity and relaxed friendliness remain the hallmarks of this roadside institution.

## IT'S THE WOOD THAT MAKES IT GOOD

It's quite a sight to behold the flames dancing up out of the eighteen-foot-long, three-foot-wide cinder-block wood pit that is the centerpiece of The Place. At any given time, a half dozen or more college-student-age cooks are jockeying their orders in wire baskets and grates suspended over the flames, then scurrying the hot, roasted goodies to diners' tables. It's kind of like being at a big Boy Scout cookout—except the food is much, much better.

The fire pit itself is fed with planks of local hardwood from a mill several miles away in rural North Guilford. The mill sells the outer slabs of lumber by the cord to Gary and Vaughn, and there's always a good-sized pile nearby that's ready to toss into the pit. All the cooks wear heavy-duty, fire-retardant gloves to handle the sizzling-hot racks, and some (not all) of the food is removed from the racks and plated before being brought to your table. The faint, pleasant smell of wood smoke permeates the air, giving a cozy campfire feel to The Place, even in the middle of a summer heat wave.

Vaughn and Gary readily admit that, if they went before Guilford's zoning board today to try to start a restaurant like The Place, there's no way they would be allowed to do what they do. (They've been grandfathered in for many years,

### Put Your Rump on a Stump

Perhaps the most unique thing about The Place is the seating. It's all on tree stumps provided by a local woodcutter, and fifty to sixty stumps are replaced each year as the older stumps begin to show their age. Gary and Vaughn paint the names of their most loyal customers on select stumps. Once you become a regular at The Place and you're deemed "stumpworthy" by the Knowles brothers, a stump will be named in your honor.

The brightly painted red plywood table tops are also mounted on tree stumps, adding to the woodsy, casual feel of the place. You're welcome to bring your own tablecloth and place settings, if you wish, and some regulars have rather elaborate setups that they bring with them for visits to The Place. In the event of rain, a huge circus-type tarp suspended on a wire between two poles is hoisted over the dining area, providing a dry (if somewhat smoky) dining experience.

keeping them immune from many of the town's more contemporary zoning requirements.) This means there's very little they can change about their setup, and that's fine with them.

## |||||||||| TWO MUST-HAVES ||||||||||
## |||||||||| FROM THE PIT ||||||||||

There are two things you absolutely must try when you visit The Place: the roasted clams and the fire-roasted corn on the cob. Good-sized littleneck clams are roasted over the open fire on a metal screen until they pop open. You may have them with or without the signature cocktail sauce applied during the cooking process. When ready, they're delivered sizzling hot to your table, metal screen and all. Once they've cooled a bit, you may use little wooden forks to scoop them out, or you may do as the regulars do: slurp the clams directly from their warm shells then discard the shells on the ground—a time-honored custom at The Place.

As for the corn on the cob, the native corn is left in its husk, and a dozen or so ears at a time are placed in wire baskets and suspended over the pit. The husks literally catch fire and get completely charred in the process, sending cinders into the warm updrafts above. When the corn is done, a cook deftly shucks the ears using special gloves, dunks them in a vat of melted butter, and sends them your way on a floppy paper plate. Prepare yourself for a little slice of heaven—fire-roasted corn is definitely the way to go.

This may be the only place in New England (or anywhere, for that matter) where you can

**THE** Place's famous fire pit is stoked with local timber.

get a fire-roasted lobster, and it's an unforgettable experience. The lobster meat comes out tender and smoky flavored, and a generous dish of melted butter is served on the side. A number of other menu items, such as bluefish, catfish, salmon, shrimp, and chicken, are wrapped in foil and placed over the pit, which seals in the juices. There's also a tasty veggie kabob featuring a variety of roasted, marinated vegetables.

## YALE'S BACKYARD

The Place does a lot of business with various groups from nearby Yale University. Fraternities, sororities, academic departments, sports teams, choirs—you name it, virtually every type of group on the Bulldog campus makes its way to The Place at some time or other for a meal under the stars. So, if you want to get a glimpse of the Ivy League letting its hair down, this is a good place to do it. (Speaking of bulldogs, your canine companions are welcome at The Place as long as they are well behaved. Fido may curl up under your table and enjoy the dinner scene, just like at home.)

Above and beyond its unique menu, setting, and cast of characters (workers and patrons alike), what really makes The Place special is the friendly, casual, backyard-type atmosphere that pervades the entire scene all summer long. Dining outdoors in a relaxed, funky setting instantly puts people in a good mood, and there's lots of spirited chatter and laughter in the air at all times. The Knowles have created a one-of-a-kind eatery with one-of-a-kind food, and the clam-loving world is all the better for it.

## The Best Non-Fried Clams on Earth

Most clam shacks specialize in frying up their battered or breaded clams in hot oil. Not so at The Place. There's nary a deep fryer on the premises. The best and most famous clams at The Place are those that are roasted over an open fire. They also serve steamed clams.

The Place's roasted clams are known far and wide for their unique smoky flavor. They have won the enduring high honor of "Best Non-Fried Clams on Earth" from the venerable website www.weloveclams.com, created and maintained by big-time clam aficionado Michael N. Marcus.

# Lenny and Joe's Fish Tale

**1301 Boston Post Road, Madison, CT 06443 | (203) 245-7289 | www.ljfishtale.com | Open year-round**

The tony shoreline town of Madison, Connecticut, is home to renowned chef Jacques Pepin (a major fried-clam lover himself), top-notch independent bookstore RJ Julia, and the largest and most popular beach on Connecticut's side of Long Island Sound: Hammonasset Beach State Park. Thousands of people flock to the park each summer to take in the sun and sand, to hike the short but scenic trails, and to pitch tents and park trailers in Hammonasset's vast campground facilities. So, it's only natural that certain enterprising individuals would eventually set up fried seafood stands just outside the park to cater to all the hungry beachgoers on the hot days and cool nights of summer.

## MEET LENNY AND JOE

Perhaps the area's most enterprising and successful fried-clam entrepreneurs are brothers Lenny and Joe Goldberg, who opened their original drive-in stand with four picnic tables and a screened-in porch just east of Hammonasset on U.S. 1 in 1979. After graduating from college, the brothers cast about for a good business to go into together. Neither had marketable degrees (both were poli-sci majors), and since both of them had toiled in food service jobs while students, they hit upon the idea of opening a restaurant. Their kitchens became test labs where they perfected seafood recipes, and they traveled around the country, sampling seafood at a variety of restaurants and drive-ins. When

**LENNY** and Joe's ever-busy order counter.

they found the right spot on the Connecticut shore to open a restaurant and the right menu to serve up to the summertime crowd, Lenny and Joe's Fish Tale was born.

Over the years, Lenny and Joe's has grown into a legendary Connecticut shoreline eatery with legions of seafood lovers and a core following that extends across as many as three generations of shoreline families. It's not unusual to see grandparents, parents, and kids sharing a meal at Lenny and Joe's, upholding a tradition that looks like it'll be around for many years to come.

The Lenny and Joe's of today in Madison retains many of its original shack qualities (ordering and picking up food from the counter, picnic table seating outdoors, oversized portions of deep-fried seafood platters, boiled lobster, ice cream, etc). Plus, it now has plenty of indoor seating, with numerous booths in a dining room across from the counter and in a large enclosed porch.

The Fish Tale can accommodate around 100 hungry customers indoors on a rainy or cold day. But the real action is outside on the gravel-bedded sea of picnic tables, where there is a combination ice-cream and gift stand and a delightful wooden carousel that takes kids for rides during the summer season. It costs a dollar to ride the carousel, and all proceeds go to local charitable

## Lenny and Joe's Coleslaw

This simple recipe yields an excellent batch of the Fish Tale's famous coleslaw for your enjoyment at home or on a picnic. Give it a try!

INGREDIENTS

¼ cup sugar

1 teaspoon salt

1 teaspoon celery seed

1 head cabbage (shredded)

1 small red pepper (chopped)

1 carrot (shredded)

¼ purple onion (chopped)

⅔ cup mayonnaise

2 tablespoons white vinegar

In a large mixing bowl, pour the sugar, salt, and celery seed over the cabbage, red pepper, carrot, and purple onion. Let stand for 15 minutes. Add the mayonnaise and vinegar and mix well.

causes and organizations. Since the Goldbergs began the charity rides concept in 1999, the carousel has raised over $600,000.

## WHAT'S COOKIN' AT THE TALE?

Over the years, the two brothers have perfected their recipes and expanded their menu, but they've never strayed very far from the deep fryers that put them on the map some thirty years ago. Breaded, fried seafood still dominates the menu offerings, and they've set a standard by which all fried seafood is measured up and down the Connecticut shore and even over the border into Rhode Island. The deep-fried fish and shellfish are made to order and lightly breaded so the oil doesn't linger. Each order is quickly immersed in a succession of two fryers for quick, clean cooking that locks in the flavor and keeps the grease from soaking in. The whole-belly clams and the fillet of sole are remarkable, as are the fresh fried sea scallops, which are locally sourced.

THERE'S plenty to do at Lenny and Joe's.

Many of the seafood platters are offered in regular and super sizes. A word to the wise (and the calorie-conscious): stick with the regular-sized platters. The super-sized ones are so ridiculously large that you'll be embarrassed when they haul it out and place it in front of you. They are, however, appropriate for those who like to share.

The best-selling item at Lenny and Joe's doesn't come anywhere near the deep-fryers. The Fish Tale's warm, buttery lobster rolls are the restaurant's most popular item, year in and year out. The roll consists of 100 percent lobster meat (no celery, no mayo), served warm and drizzled with butter on a hot, top-split, lightly buttered and toasted bun. It's a bit messy but oh-so-good.

Speaking of lobster, for years Lenny and Joe's has operated a seasonal lobster stand on the outdoor porch. They recently built a small expansion onto their kitchen and brought the lobster stand indoors where it is now a year-round operation. You may get a lobster dinner, which features a 1⅛-pound steamed lobster, corn on the cob, salt potatoes, and drawn butter, or double your fun with a twin lobster dinner. The Fish Tale Lobster Feast includes a cup of chowder, a quart of steamed clams, lobster, corn, salt potatoes, and butter. In addition, there are king crab and grilled salmon dinners in a variety of combinations with or without lobster.

## SOME HEART-HEALTHY CHOICES

The Fish Tale has been ahead of the curve when it comes to offering healthy alternatives to deep-fried fare. For years (particularly at their delightful sit-down restaurant in nearby West-brook) they have offered an array of baked and broiled seafood dishes, often served with fresh steamed vegetables. Some of these dishes (particularly the casserole ones) have butter in them, so you may instead wish to opt for the excellent broiled fish fillets.

Lenny and Joe's grinds and prepares its own coleslaw daily, and it's a delightful complement to nearly every meal on the menu. And there's an excellent alternative to the tasty french fries and onion rings: boiled salt potatoes. These small red taters are boiled for just the right amount of time in briny salted water, and they go well with just about everything on the menu.

## The Fish Tale Clam Chowder (Home Version)

In many ways, you can judge a clam shack by its chowder, and Lenny and Joe's makes an excellent one. The Fish Tale's chowder is the clear-broth variety, which is usually associated with Rhode Island shacks. There's a touch of evaporated milk added for sweetness, but no actual milk, half-and-half, or heavy cream. And the recipe calls for fresh quahog clams, shucked and chopped into small pieces. Making this chowder takes some effort, but the reward on the gustatory side is well worth it. This recipe makes approximately 10 to 12 servings.

INGREDIENTS

- ¾ pound salt pork
- ½ cup diced onion
- 8 pounds fresh quahog clams
- 2½ quarts water
- 6 pounds chef potatoes, peeled and diced
- ½ cup chopped celery

13-ounce can of evaporated milk

Salt and white pepper to taste

Render the salt port in a large frying pan over medium heat. Remove the solids. Add the onions to the rendered salt pork liquid and cook on low heat until the onions are transparent.

Open the quahog clams with a clam knife. Save the clam juice. Chop the meat of the clams into small pieces. Set aside the chopped clam meat.

In a large stock pot, combine the water, the clam juice, the salt pork with the onions, the diced potatoes, and the chopped celery. Simmer until the potatoes are soft. Add the chopped clams to the stock, simmering until the clams are just tender.

Remove the chowder from the heat. Stir in the evaporated milk. Season to taste with the salt and pepper, and serve. (If you are going to cool the chowder down to reheat later, hold off on adding the evaporated milk until reheating the chowder in order to avoid curdling.)

## T-SHIRT DIPLOMACY

Many clam shacks sell T-shirts with their names and logos on them, but Lenny and Joe's has taken its T-shirt business to amazing heights. In 1980, they started buying factory-second T-shirts, and they printed their Fish Tale name and logo on them. Then they switched to factory-firsts and kept the price low—initially $2, then $5, and now around $6. They sell approximately 35,000 shirts per year, and at any given time there are hundreds of thousands of them in circulation.

Each year, the Fish Tale designs several new T-shirts, and some customers collect them like baseball cards. At Lenny and Joe's full-service restaurant in Westbrook, there's a "T-Shirt Hall of Fame" on the walls that displays photos of

customers in their Lenny and Joe's T's in all sorts of faraway and unusual locations (Antarctica, the Taj Mahal, the Great Wall of China, you name it). It's all free advertising as far as the Goldbergs are concerned, and their T-shirt diplomacy pretty much guarantees a steady flow of curious new customers who want to know what all the fuss is about.

So, if you happen to visit Lenny and Joe's on a busy summer weekend and you take in the crowded, theme-park-like scene with the acre or so of outdoor seating, the colorful carousel, and the busy ice-cream stand, it may be hard to imagine that this super-busy restaurant was once a modest shack with just four picnic tables in a screened-in porch. But once you become familiar with the bonhomie, passion, and commitment that the brothers Goldberg bring to their establishment and to their community, you'll understand why Lenny and Joe's Fish Tale has become a Connecticut shoreline clam shack institution with few peers. Long live Lenny and Joe's!

**LENNY** and Joe's carousel has raised hundreds of thousands of dollars for charities.

# The Clam Castle

1324 Boston Post Road, Madison, CT 06443 | (203) 245-4911 | Open early April to early October

Just up the road and across the street from Lenny and Joe's is a quintessentially vintage clam shack from days gone by: Madison's famed Clam Castle. From its quaint signage to its side-porch-style dining room to its sheltered backyard picnic tables with funky plastic clamshell strings of lights, the Clam Castle delivers not only the clams but a heaping portion of character, nostalgia, and atmosphere at the same time.

## A Throwback Shack

Founded some fifty years ago in the early 1960s by a man known only as "Art" to current and former customers and employees, the Clam Castle appears to have changed little in half a century. With its brightly painted yellow dining room, molded-plastic red booths, and window-unit air conditioner humming away in the back wall, any pretensions quickly disappear once you step inside. When you make your way to the order counter, take your time and peruse the equally bright-yellow order menu posted on the wall. While you're pondering the choices, you'll most likely hear the friendly chatter and rock music that emanates from the kitchen, which is hidden from view around the wall behind the counter. Once you've decided on what to get, place your order and then grab a seat. The counter staff will deliver your food to your table when it's ready. So goes the drill at the Clam Castle, where informality is the rule of the day.

IT'S hard to miss the Clam Castle from the highway.

Current manager George Arena is an affable man with a twinkle in his eye and an obvious passion for running the Clam Castle in the same manner that it has been run for lo these many years. When he's not working (and he works *a lot*), he likes to hop on an old bicycle he keeps stashed out back and take short rides through nearby Hammonassett Beach State Park. When he first started managing the Castle eight years ago, he was working 100-hour weeks in order to keep things humming. He has since brought his sons in to help with the cooking, allowing him to cut back to more reasonable fifty- to sixty-hour work weeks. (Such hours are not unusual for shack owners and managers during the summer season.)

## No-Nonsense Seafood Fare

The Clam Castle's menu is quite simple and straightforward—mostly seafood of the deep-fried variety with a few broiled dishes and a short list of grilled burgers, hot dogs, and

**THE** Clam Castle's portions are more than generous.

sandwiches. The namesake clams are the most popular item on the menu. Whole bellies are plentiful, on the smallish side, tender, juicy, and flavorful without being overpowering. So, if you haven't partaken of whole-belly clams before, the Castle's clams are a great place to become indoctrinated.

The clam strips are also on the petite side, but there are plenty of them, and they're cooked just right, with a light crunch as you bite in and chewy without being rubbery. When you order a platter of whole bellies or strips, you have a choice between fries and onion rings—go for the rings. The Castle hand-cuts their super thin rings, then lightly breads them and fries them to a light, crisp, golden perfection. Unlike other places where the sheer size and weight of the onion rings can be overwhelming, the Castle's rings instead leave you feeling satisfied, not stuffed.

Other deep-fried offerings include shrimp, scallops, calamari, and cod, the Castle's fish fillet of choice. Soft-shell crab is also available in season. The prices on the platters are all quite reasonable, except perhaps for the pricey Fisherman's Platter. But it contains six different types of seafood and is plenty more than enough for two people, so if you don't mind sharing with one of your dining partners, it's actually quite a bargain.

THE Castle's playful menu and wall art.

Broiled cod, sea scallops, shrimp, or a combination of all three are done with a bit of Italian flair, with lemon juice, butter, garlic, and a sprinkling of parmesan cheese on top. And don't forget the homemade clam chowder, which comes in creamy New England and clear-broth Rhode Island styles. There's also a tasty lobster bisque and fish chowder that more than hold their own against other chowders and bisques on the Connecticut shore. If you're having trouble choosing between these, go with the Rhode Island clam chowder. If you love the flavor of clams yet don't want to fill up on a heavier, cream-based chowder or bisque, a cup of the clear-broth chowder is a happy alternative and an excellent complement to any of the seafood platters.

There are plenty of fine seafood restaurants up and down the Connecticut shore, yet few these days deliver the authentic, old-time shack experience that may be had at the humble, colorful Clam Castle in Madison. Check it out and experience an authentic roadside fried seafood stand in the style and manner that made places like the Clam Castle distinctive American icons of yesteryear.

## Dozens of Da Vincis

While you're waiting for your food, take in the dozens of hand-colored Clam Castle placemats that have been affixed to just about every square inch of the walls and ceilings in the dining area. Kids (and adults) love to try their hands at coloring in and embellishing the Castle's mascot clam, which is outlined on the mat, and manager George Arena proudly displays even the most rough and humble of renderings. In addition, one wall has an aquatic mural, painted by a summer staffer a couple of years ago, that shows a school of tropical fish swimming by. So, although Long Island Sound is about half a mile from the Clam Castle, you certainly feel a lot closer to the sea with all the wonderful artwork around you.

# Johnny Ad's Drive-In

**M**ost clam shacks in New England are located close to the beach or nestled next to the town harbor or sometimes tucked away on a pleasant, winding, two-lane road not far from the sea. Not Johnny Ad's. This place sits brazenly on a busy, four-lane stretch of U.S. 1, with cars and trucks roaring by—a fair distance from the scenic beaches and harbors in the pretty little shoreline town of Old Saybrook, Connecticut.

**JOHNNY** Ad's Drive-In, in all its faded glory.

## AN ACTUAL 1950S DRIVE-IN

This faded blue shack has been around since 1957, when it was opened by John Adinopfa (aka Johnny Ad) and his wife, Hilda. The couple ran the place in pretty much the same drive-in roadside shack fashion from the 1950s until the 1990s, when current co-owner Bob Hansen leased the place from the Adinopfas.

Bob had to agree to a couple of key stipulations that came with leasing Johnny Ad's. First, he and his wife Kathleen both had to run the place together, just like Johnny and Hilda had done for decades. Second, as long as the Adinopfas actually continued to own the business, everything had to stay exactly the same as it had always been—the menu, the décor, the building, *everything*.

Bob says the first year was pretty rough. He and Kathleen had extensive experience in the hospitality and food businesses, but it was more in the corporate realm. Running a clam shack in the dead of winter on a snowy stretch of U.S. 1 in eastern Connecticut could have easily turned into something akin to *The Shining* for a couple less passionate and committed than the Hansens were to the spirit and success of the business.

Bob and Kathleen persevered and came to love their new life at Johnny Ad's, becoming the owners in 2006. They've since taken longtime employee Tenzin Lama and his wife Tsultim on as co-owners.

## ||||||| The Lay of the Land |||||||

The lack of any major change to Johnny Ad's over the last few decades is immediately apparent when you pull up in front and behold the faded original signs on the shack's roof and façade. When you enter through the front door, you find yourself in a narrow enclosed porch area with two windows opening into the busy kitchen. There's a menu made of plastic push-letters in felt sealed in a glass case on the wall between the windows. Handwritten daily specials are taped alongside.

Once your order is placed and you've received your claim ticket, you may retreat to the adjacent cozy dining room. Be sure to check out the historical photos of Johnny Ad's that hang on the walls. In good weather, head out to the numerous picnic tables with umbrellas extending off the side of the building. Tinny loudspeakers indoors and out keep the 1950s alive at Ad's, with hits from the Eisenhower era playing constantly. The staff occasionally cuts into the

## (Happily) Frozen in Time

Upon taking ownership of the drive-in, Bob Hansen toyed with the idea of tearing down Johnny Ad's and putting up something more substantial on the Route 1 lot. But the uniqueness of the place and the strong loyalty of the customers, who didn't want him to change a thing, caused him to reconsider. (Local zoning laws also gave him pause, as Johnny Ad's was basically grandfathered into its current location on a wedge of land backed by a nearby residential neighborhood.)

Time went by and the atmosphere of the drive-in continued to grow on him, so he made the decision to stand pat and forge ahead as the Johnny Ad's that everyone knows and loves. (The Hansens have since added to their local restaurant portfolio, opening the British-style Penny Lane Pub on Main Street in Old Saybrook a few years ago.)

**JOHNNY** Ad's in the 1950s.

tunes with crackling announcements for food orders ready to be picked up.

## What Makes Johnny's Famous

Probably the most popular and best-known dish at Johnny Ad's is the hot buttered lobster roll. Served in classic Connecticut style, it features large chunks of warm, hand-picked lobster meat drizzled with melted butter, which soaks into the top-split bun, making a messy yet tasty treat, especially when enjoyed with the homemade coleslaw. Bob takes great pride in the fact that the buns literally disintegrate under the weight of the lobster meat and the warmth of the butter as you dig into your roll. The regulars at Johnny Ad's wouldn't have it any other way.

The seafood platter is another popular dish, with its array of lightly breaded and fried clams, shrimp, scallops, and fish, accompanied by french fries and dollops of cold lobster salad

**NANCY** Darrow, the heart and soul of Johnny Ad's.

and coleslaw on the side. This is a belt buster, and you may wish to split it with one of your traveling companions.

One other item that really brings 'em in is the famous foot-long hot dog. This bad boy is grilled, not boiled, and you may have it smothered in chili and chopped raw onion, if you so desire. (Writer Dominic Dunne, who lived for years in nearby Hadlyme, used to stop in for a foot-long whenever he was in Old Saybrook.) The wieners are Hummels, a regionally famous brand out of New Haven. As if all this seafood and hot dog nostalgia isn't enough, there's a small, seasonal ice-cream stand on the premises, serving cones, dishes, sundaes, milk shakes, and other frozen treats.

The next time you're flying along on the Boston Post Road in Old Saybrook, do yourself a favor by detouring into this roadside delight and have a meal that will make you yearn for simpler, happier, tastier times.

# The Hallmark Drive-In

113 Shore Road, Old Lyme, CT 06371 | (860) 434-1998 | Open April to November

If you happen to be heading northeast on I-95 in eastern Connecticut, there's a nice detour to take once you've crossed over the Connecticut River. Take the first exit after the bridge, and bear right onto Route 156, which quickly turns into a bucolic country road running parallel to the mouth of the river and Long Island Sound as you head south and east through Old Lyme. After motoring along for a few miles, you'll come across the Hallmark Drive-In on the right-hand side—you can easily spot it by its quaint rooftop signage and the lines snaking from the order window out into the parking lot in front.

Although known primarily as an ice-cream stand on Old Lyme's scenic shore road, there is plenty of deep-fried and grilled seafood here to warrant a visit for lunch or dinner in spring, summer, or fall. You may initially come to the Hallmark for the homemade ice cream, but you'll end up staying for the tasty victuals.

## One Hundred Years and Counting

Owners Gary and Peggy Legein have been stewards of the Hallmark for the past ten years, and they presided over the venerable stand as it recently celebrated its 100th birthday. The Hallmark was originally located about two miles from its current location, and it initially served just ice cream and homemade chocolates. In the 1970s, the stand moved to its current location, and it began serving food in addition to sweets. Deep-fried clams were a natural, given the Hallmark's proximity to the Sound, and they were an immediate hit with

**THE** Hallmark is famous for its homemade ice cream.

the locals. Other seafood items, such as clam strips, scallops, crab cakes, shrimp, and fish and chips have been added over the years, elevating the Hallmark from a mere ice-cream stand to full shack status. The Legeins recently changed

## It's All About the View

Whether you opt for seafood, a sandwich, or ice cream at the Hallmark Drive-In, when your number is called and you pick up your goodies from the window, head around the corner of the stand to the umbrellaed tables that await you in back, and feast your eyes on the lovely field of marsh grass that extends unimpeded for several hundred yards all the way to Long Island Sound. It's truly a serene setting, and diners have been known to linger long after their meals and snacks are done, as it's hard to tear yourself away from such a peaceful and scenic place.

If you can't find a spot out back, there are several shaded picnic tables bordering the eastern edge of the Hallmark lot, and they provide a pleasant respite of their own. Or, if you're feeling social and only have an ice-cream cone in hand, feel free to mingle with the locals out front while they wait in line to order or pick up. There's something about Old Lyme that puts most people in a friendly sort of way. (It probably has something to do with the Hallmark's ice cream!)

their deep-fried seafood recipe to batter dipping, combined with a fine coating of finely ground cracker crumbs. The result is heavenly.

Equally popular are the foot-long hot dogs and the grilled burgers, which come in an amazing variety of styles and patty numbers (a single-, double-, and even a triple-patty burger for the truly famished). Gary often recommends to his younger patrons that they consider splitting a foot-long instead of getting one apiece, as more often than not, the tykes can't finish the entire thing. How's that for putting people before profit?

The hot dogs are grilled and served on a split-top bun, in keeping with the New England tradition. You may, of course, get a healthy dollop of chili, onion, and/or cheese on your dog, if you wish.

Seafood rolls come in the usual varieties, and the lobster salad roll is served cold, in contrast to many of the rest of Connecticut's shacks, which serve them with warm lobster meat and melted butter. There are also grinders, deli sandwiches, grilled cheeses, and several interesting and unusual chicken sandwich creations served either grilled or fried.

But the big deal here is still the ice cream. It's made fresh daily on the premises in a large ice-cream churning machine in back. There are some twenty-five regular flavors on the menu

**THE** Hallmark boasts an excellent outdoor dining area.

and several daily special flavors, which are made fresh and served on a rotating basis. The ice cream's not cheap, but it's oh-so-good. You can really taste the fresh, home-churned texture and flavor in every lick or bite.

## A MAGNET FOR CELEBRITIES

Don't be fooled by the sleepy appearance of Old Lyme. It's always drawn famous people looking to get away from the crowds of not-too-distant New York City. You never know with whom you may find yourself standing in line while you're waiting to order your ice cream or clams.

Gary and Peggy say that Old Lyme resident and best-selling author Luanne Rice is a frequent customer who has paid homage to the Hallmark in her novels through her fictional Paradise Ice Cream Stand, which appears in a number of her works. Sally Jessy Raphael also lives nearby and likes to stop in for some fresh ice cream from time to time. Once, a fleet of sleek sports cars pulled in and around the side

of the building and parked in a shady spot in back. Out popped Ralph Lauren and his entourage for a quick bite to eat. They didn't leave disappointed. And master chef Bobby Flay showed up at the order window one night, to find that the Hallmark had closed and only the starstruck cleaning crew remained inside, unable to cook him any clams or dish him up any ice cream that evening. (Come back, Bobby, you'll be glad you did!)

On the non-celebrity front, but just as impressive, was a newlywed couple a few years ago who insisted that they and all their invited wedding guests stop at the Hallmark for some ice cream between the wedding ceremony and the reception. Some 140 celebrants were served Hallmark's finest before continuing on to the reception hall. There may have been nary a celebrity in that crowd, but there was certainly a lot of love for that little, more-than-100-year-old stand on the quiet, scenic road in beautiful Old Lyme.

# Fred's Shanty

**272 Pequot Avenue, New London, CT 06320 | (860) 447-1301 | www.fredsshanty.com
Open mid-March to mid-October**

**N**ew London, Connecticut, has a long and colorful maritime history. Once a major whaling port, this small city on the Thames River is home to the U.S. Coast Guard Academy, the Eugene O'Neill Theater Center (O'Neill spent lots of time in New London as a youth), and Connecticut College. Across the river in the town of Groton is the famed U.S. naval submarine base, which serves as home for the USS *Nautilus*, the world's first nuclear submarine (it's open for tours). New London is in the midst of a long, steady renaissance, with restaurants and cultural attractions sprouting up throughout the city as people rediscover the charming old houses and buildings around town and the lovely seaside location.

Then there's popular Ocean Beach, which is reached by navigating your way through town on a two-lane road paralleling the Thames and going by the stately homes of nineteenth-century whaling captains. Along this route, keep your eyes peeled on the river side of the road for a modest drive-in clam shack known as Fred's Shanty, housed in a low-slung building that literally hangs over the edge of a large pleasure-craft dock along the banks of the river.

## AN IMMEDIATE HIT

Fred's has been feeding seafood-hungry New Londoners and beachgoers since 1972 when local restaurateur Fred Poulos opened his eponymous shack. Its casual, open-air setup facing

**FRED'S** Shanty sits cheek-by-jowl with the Thames River in New London.

directly onto busy Pequot Avenue, just a quarter mile from Eugene O'Neill's boyhood summer home and a mile or so from Ocean Beach, made it immediately accessible to neighborhood denizens and beachgoers alike. Word spread, and Fred's was off and running, a welcome addition to the New London waterfront scene.

John Hefferman, who hails from the nearby town of Waterford, worked in various restaurants as a teenager. Then he managed Fred's from 1988 to 1992 before taking a sales job in the South. When John heard that Poulos was putting the shack up for sale in 2000, he immediately came back and bought it, and he has been the happy owner ever since. John's sister and brother-in-law and a few other family members pitch in and help run Fred's, along with a staff of about twenty-five part-timers working in various shifts throughout the busy summer months.

## A TRUE NEIGHBORHOOD SHACK

What's neat about Fred's is that it seems to get about as many walk-in customers as it does drive-ins, lending a real neighborhood feel to the place. The Shanty is right up against Pequot Avenue in a mixed residential and business stretch of the road, and it's tightly woven into the fabric of the neighborhood as both a place to grab a bite and as a meeting place for residents,

**JOHN** Hefferman, Fred's owner.

students, and workers from nearby companies. (Pfizer and General Dynamics have large operations nearby, supplying Fred's with a steady flow of lunchtime customers.)

Fred's menu is very basic, serving deep-fried seafood, burgers, and hot dogs as well as soft-serve ice cream and Hershey's hard-packed ice cream in cones and cups. The best-selling items are the clam strips and the tasty fish sandwich. Flounder is the fish of choice here—lightly breaded and served in small, strip-like portions that fit easily onto a bun. The clam strips are also small and very chewy and tasty—better than the larger strips you find at many other establishments.

The whole bellies run a close third place to the clam strips and fish. They're very clean and tasty with no trace of grit when you bite in. The sizeable sea scallops are cut in half, breaded, and fried into bite-sized chunks. And Fred's serves a surprisingly nice calamari that's salty, sweet, and light. It's great as a snack or as the centerpiece of a calamari dinner plate with fries and homemade coleslaw. Prices on all the seafood dishes are very reasonable, which is always a plus, especially if you're footing the bill to feed your family for lunch or dinner. John changes the vegetable oil in his fryers twice daily, guaranteeing an excellent finished product.

**DEEP-FRIED** seafood rules at Fred's Shanty.

## |||||| SANDWICHES AND ROLLS |||||

The grill at Fred's keeps very busy throughout the day with burgers and foot-long hot dogs. The wieners are one of Fred's best-selling items, and there are frequent specials on them, such as buy two and get the third free (check ahead for daily and seasonal specials). The lobster roll is of the cold-meat variety, mixed with mayo and served on a bed of lettuce in a split-top bun. Various grilled chicken and chicken tender items round out the simple yet satisfying non-seafood items on the menu.

Although you can get your food to go, it's best enjoyed curbside at one of the dozen or so tables under awnings and umbrellas on either side of the shack. You have a commanding view of the street scene out front and the harbor on the Thames in back. Fred's is a very social place, so don't be surprised if you get pulled into a conversation with neighboring diners. Oldies music blares pleasantly from outdoor speakers, adding to the good cheer of the entire scene.

Fred's is a hard-working, no-nonsense shack that's open seven days a week from mid-March to mid-October. Although it looks diminutive, a lot of seafood, burgers, and hot dogs move through this place all season long. It's a testament to the fact that the simple pleasures of a good meal with some fine company in friendly surroundings can make any day a little brighter.

# Costello's Clam Shack

**145 Pearl Street, Noank, CT 06340 | (860) 572-2779 | www.costellosclamshack.com**
**Open late May to early September**

Costello's Clam Shack is housed in a blue-and-white-canopied, two-story building perched at the end of a pier in the picturesque harbor of Noank, Connecticut. Noank is a quiet, colonial seaside borough just a bit south and west of Mystic, Connecticut, home of the famed Mystic Seaport and Mystic Aquarium (and the setting for the 1980s Julia Roberts movie *Mystic Pizza*). Noank has all the charm of its larger neighbor, yet it has been spared much of the noise and congestion that one frequently finds in Mystic during the busy summer season.

It's a bit of a challenge to find Costello's. After you make your way down Noank's quaint, narrow streets lined with lovely 200-year-old framed houses (and street pavement ribbed with numerous speed bumps—an important clue that you're getting close), you drive fifty yards or so past Abbott's

**THE** smiling, happy crew at Costello's.

Lobster in the Rough, then take a left into the Noank Harbor parking lot, which is populated equally with parked cars and dry-docked boats. You can just see a bit of Costello's poking out at the end of the dock straight ahead—just make your way out to the blue-and-white-striped canopies at the end of the dock, and get in line in front of the order window.

## What, No Deep Fryers?!

Costello's is the brainchild of Jerry and Dierdre Mears, the father-and-daughter team that owns nearby Abbott's Lobster in the Rough, a restaurant famed for its steamed and boiled lobster and steamed clams and for its wonderful outdoor dining "in the rough" by the harbor. Customers over the years at Abbott's kept asking for deep-fried clams and other seafood, but Jerry and Dierdre didn't want to complicate their simple, classic lobster

## Abbott's Lobster in the Rough

Just up the road from Costello's is the clam shack's big brother, Abbott's Lobster in the Rough. (Abbott's and Costello's—get it?)

Abbott's is certainly the more famous of the two eateries—a storied lobster pound that draws huge crowds throughout the summer to dine on boiled and steamed lobster and clams while gazing out at lovely Noank harbor; it's just several boat slips north of Costello's. (There's a longstanding tradition among local boaters to pull up to the docks in front of Abbott's or Costello's, tie up, and come ashore for lunch or dinner.)

Abbott's and Costello's owner Jerry Mears got things started when he opened Abbott's over fifty years ago. Since then, the famous lobster pound has served up more than a million lobsters on its spacious grounds where you'll find bright red picnic tables in and around the main building and out on the spacious dock that protrudes into the harbor. There's also an ice-cream stand and a souvenir shop on the premises.

Abbott's is open May through Columbus Day and is located at 117 Pearl Street in Noank; (860) 536-5763; www. abbotts-lobster.com.

pound setup with deep-fried fare. So, they hit upon the idea of opening a separate clam shack, and they found a spot just down the road that was perfect. Thus was Costello's born.

### FRIED CLAMS AND MORE

The fun at Costello's begins when you're greeted at the order window by an always cheerful staff member, usually a high-school or college student who has one of the better summer jobs in Noank. There are a lot of seafood entrees and side dishes to choose from, so take your time and pick carefully.

For starters, you may want to consider an order of steamed clams. Harvested from Canada's Bay of Fundy, they're steamed to perfection and served with clam broth and drawn butter for varied dousings. The crispy, sweet fried calamari, served with a tangy marinara sauce, is another good opening choice.

You can't go wrong with the fried clams— whole belly or strips—for your main dish. They're battered, light, tender, and flavorful, with a delicate crunch when you bite in. The deep-fried clams also hail from Canada, and the portion sizes are generous.

Cod is the fillet of choice at Costello's, both for the batter-fried fish and chips and for the tasty fish sandwich. Other deep-fried dinners include sea scallops or shrimp, both of which are lightly breaded and seasoned before frying. The deep-fried seafood dinners come with Costello's famous crispy, crunchy french fries. They're thin-cut and batter-fried for an extra pleasing crunchy texture. The wide-cut onion rings are breaded before frying and make for a great side dish or appetizer. Creamy coleslaw comes with each of the dinner plates as well.

With Abbott's right next door, you might think Costello's would demur and shy away from anything having to do with lobster. Think again. Costello's lobster rolls contain a quarter-pound of fresh-picked lobster meat and may be had either hot and drenched in butter or cold with a special dressing and chunks of celery. Both versions are served on a toasted roll and come with potato chips and coleslaw. Costello's also offers what they call Noank-style chowder—a clear-broth version that's light, hearty, and packed with fresh-clam flavor.

## Come for the Food, Stay for the View

Perhaps the best thing about Costello's is the magnificent view from the open-air upper deck, which overlooks Noank harbor, home to everything from one-person dinghies to 100-foot yachts. Grab a table on the rail if you can and gaze out on the scene before you. When the sun is shining, a light breeze is blowing,

**ONE** artist's interpretation of the fun to be had at Costello's.

and the water sparkles with a light chop, there aren't many places on the New England coast as serene as this. Costello's is a BYOB operation, so feel free to bring a bottle of wine for sipping while you take in the beautiful view.

Like most good shacks, Costello's can get very busy and crowded at lunch and dinner hours and pretty much all day on weekends. But if you hit this place on the right day at the right time, with a soft breeze blowing in from the sea and the sunlight sparkling on the water, Costello's and its fine food and atmosphere can transport your weary soul (and appetite) to a very happy place indeed.

# The Sea View

**145 Greenmanville Avenue, Mystic, CT 06355 | (860) 572-0096 | Open April to early November**

**S**ome New England eateries are strategically located to take full advantage of the tourist traffic that flows to and from nearby attractions, and the Sea View of Mystic is a perfect example of this intentional (perhaps incidental) marketing strategy. Situated on the only road that runs between the popular Mystic Aquarium and its maritime counterpart, Mystic Seaport, the Sea View is guaranteed to have a steady stream of traffic (and hungry customers) passing by all day long in spring, summer, and fall.

**THE** Sea View on a sunny summer day.

As you're driving by, it's hard to resist the quaint, wooden, brightly painted aquamarine shack, with its playful octopus signage and its clusters of shaded and open-air picnic tables on the banks of the Mystic River harbor. This place all but screams for you to stop in, check out the view, and enjoy a basket of fried seafood while you're there.

## It's All in the Family

Shack owner/operators Bill Botchis and his daughter Angela Baton have been in business since the bicentennial year of 1976. Angela says the original shack was so small that the half-dozen family members working inside during those initial busy seasons were packed together so tightly they couldn't move around while they were working. Everyone had a set position and performed one task to minimize the jostling. An eventual shack expansion alleviated the phone-booth-type space problem. (It still isn't very large.)

So far, three generations of Bill's Italian/Greek family have worked at Sea View over the years. The family supplements its labor needs in the busy season primarily by hiring hardworking exchange students from eastern Europe, Russia, and elsewhere for summertime employment and a taste of life in the United States.

This place is super busy during the summer months, as thousands of cars pass by each day on their way

**THE** Sea View's "dining room" on the banks of the Mystic River.

to and from the aquarium, the seaport, and the historic town of Mystic. Many of them stop in for lunch or dinner. If you want to avoid the most crowded times, Angela recommends a mid-afternoon visit for a more relaxing experience. Regardless, just sitting by the river and taking in the boats in the harbor is pleasant, no matter how crowded the order window may be. You can gaze upon the impressive tall ships at Mystic Seaport just downriver from the Sea View's dining area.

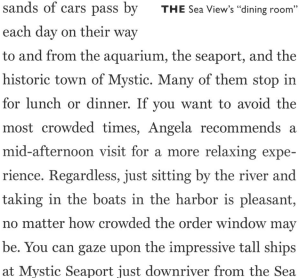

## CLAMS AND MORE

Even if you have to wait a bit for your food, it's well worth it. Perhaps the most distinctive and popular dish at the Sea View is the fried clam

plate. The clams here are small, sweet, and plentiful, and they really don't need any embellishment in the form of tartar or cocktail sauce. You can eat these little guys by the handful, savoring the light breading and the tender, flavorful clams within.

The lobster roll, another popular choice, is served cold and mixed with mayo and celery on a bed of lettuce and packed into a lightly toasted bun. The sandwich has a bit of a kick to it from some secret spice—a pleasant surprise, given that cold lobster rolls can be a bit on the bland side.

The sea scallops are from local fisheries, and they're firm, chewy, and full of that deep-sea scallop flavor. You may want these on a roll or as a platter with homemade coleslaw and fries. Crab cakes are another delight, made from hand-picked fresh crabmeat, not the frozen kind.

## THEY KEEP COMING BACK

You might think, with the transient tourist population whizzing by the Sea View's front door every day, that repeat customers might not be an important part of the business. Not so. There are families, often multigenerational, who come back year after year to enjoy at least one meal together at the picnic tables at Sea View.

When Hurricane Earl recently threatened the New England coast, winds were whipping up and rains were lashing the shack and surrounding tents. Yet one determined family of die-hard customers showed up and insisted on eating under the tent, saying they drove hundreds of miles each year to dine at Sea View as part of their annual New England vacation, and they weren't going to let a little storm spoil their fun. For a brief time the winds lashed and the rain poured down, but the hurricane stayed well

**OWNER** Angela Barton, ready to take your order.

off the coast and everyone had a fine time. Such can be the pull of a good clam shack on out-of-towners who have strong ties and fond memories of places like the Sea View.

The locals love this place, also. Employees from the aquarium and from the seaport stop in regularly for lunch, and many summer residents stop in several times per season to partake of Sea View's scrumptious fare, especially at dinnertime during weekdays. Little League and soccer teams will stop by for ice cream after games, and with uniformed youngsters running and laughing around the grounds, the small-town feel of the place is alluring.

Even if you don't plan on visiting the wonderful sites that Mystic has to offer, keep in mind that the Sea View is only a minute or so off I-95 and is a great alternative to the prepackaged fare so frequently served along the busy interstate. If you've had enough of the highway, pull into Sea View, order up a deep-fried platter, and soak up the serenity of this beautiful aquamarine shack on the shores of the Mystic River.

# The Sea Swirl

**30 Williams Avenue, Mystic CT 06355 | (860) 536-3452 | www.seaswirlofmystic.com**
**Open early April to early October**

Sea Swirl celebrated its twenty-fifth anniversary under its current ownership in 2010, and it's been a very good quarter-century for this venerable shack on the flood tide of the Mystic River in the beautiful seaside town of Mystic, Connecticut.

"The Swirl," as it's known locally, is housed in a distinctive angular glass-fronted building that used to be a Carvel Ice Cream stand. It's right up against Route 1 in front and backed up against a tire shop to the rear. Although it looks like it's a bit crowded into its little slice of the roadside, there's plenty of room for pulling in and parking, a bunch of picnic tables that nearly surround the building, and a large-size tent with more tables under it right next to the tidal basin.

## SERVING FOOD THE WAY *THEY* LIKE IT

Owners Dave and Kathleen Blaney sort of fell into the business in 1984 when they purchased the stand and started refurbishing it for their grand opening in 1985. From the beginning, the Blaneys' guiding philosophy has been to offer a dining experience in the style that they liked most—fried clams and other seafood served in a clean, friendly atmosphere at reasonable prices. "We were consumers," says Dave, "and we liked fried clams. So, we came up with recipes that pleased us, and we used them to make the food that we serve to this day."

The learning curve was pretty steep for the first couple of years. Neither Dave nor Kathleen had any formal training in the restaurant business—Dave washed dishes for a while at a deli while a student, and Kathleen's Serbo-Croatian family had a long history of running eateries, but that was about it. When they first opened Sea Swirl,

**SEA** Swirl owners Kathleen and Dave Blaney.

they had one young daughter, and another was born shortly thereafter. They fumbled their way through those early years and then hit their stride, and they haven't looked back since.

## WELL-DESERVED FAME

Sea Swirl has consistently drawn high praise from local, regional, and national media for their outstanding seafood, especially their whole-belly clams. Local food writer Lee White named Sea Swirl's clams "best of the best" in the early 1990s, which started pulling in curious locals who hadn't yet discovered the place. Jane and Michael Stern of *Road Food* fame have been fans of Sea Swirl for years. Michael once stated that Sea Swirl "has sustained a deserved reputation as one of the finest places this side of Ipswich to eat fried clams, especially the whole-belly variety." And Rachael Ray filmed a segment of her *$40 a Day* Food Network TV show at Sea Swirl several years ago. *Connecticut* magazine writes regular raves about the Swirl's food and ice cream, and the *New York Times* and *Boston Globe* have also jumped on the Sea Swirl bandwagon with glowing reviews in their papers.

What makes Sea Swirl so distinctive in the competitive fried-seafood market of southeast Connecticut? Among other things, Dave thinks it has a lot to do with two things: the locally harvested seafood and the method of preparation. "We get our cod for the fish sandwiches fresh four or five times a week from Stonington harbor," which is just up the road a few miles. Stonington is also the source for the Swirl's sea scallops. Dave often goes to the Stonington docks himself to hand-pick seafood from the day's catch, guaranteeing that he'll get the level of quality he expects.

Sea Swirl's clams come from not-too-distant New Hampshire and Maine, where the catch is plentiful and consistent. The shrimp perhaps travel farthest, coming from the Gulf of Mexico and occasionally from Venezuela. Despite the recent difficulties in the gulf, Dave insists that gulf shrimp are still the best, and many of his fellow shack owners agree.

## VARIETY FROM THE FRYERS

The other mark of distinction is Sea Swirl's variety of preparation prior to committing its seafood to the deep fryer. "The concept has been not to have everything taste the same," Dave says with a smile. He feels that, if everything were breaded or battered in the same way, there would be little to differentiate the flavor between the various dishes. So, the whole-belly clams and shrimp are dredged in flour, the clam strips and scallops in cornmeal, and the cod in wet batter. This can create some confusion in the kitchen, but the Blaneys feel it's worth the extra effort, and their success over the years has proven them out.

Of all the dishes served up at the Swirl, Dave is most proud of the battered, English-style cod, served both as a sandwich (Sea Swirl's most popular item) and as one half of its fish and chips platter. The wet batter gives the firm, white cod a distinctive crunch when you bite in, followed by a burst of fresh flavor that's sealed in by the crispy batter coating. Mmmmm, good!

Unlike many other Connecticut clam shacks, Sea Swirl serves a cold version of its lobster roll. This may be a throwback to Dave's upbringing in Boston, where cold lobster rolls generally rule. Sea Swirl's lobster meat is lightly tossed in a small amount of mayo, and small pieces of celery are blended in for flavor and crunch. A bed of lettuce and a toasted New England–style roll complete the tasty package.

## THE ICE-CREAM FACTOR

A big part of Sea Swirl's business has nothing to do with the deep fryers. True to its origins as an ice-cream stand, nearly a third of the Swirl's business is in the ice-cream trade. Soft-serve is usually the ice cream of choice here; however, hard-packed ice cream is also available in about ten different flavors.

The soft-serve may be had by cup or cone in a wide variety of flavors, toppings, and dips. Soft-serve is also the basis for Sea Swirl's sinfully large and rich sundaes, flurries, banana splits, and thick and creamy milk shakes. You may also opt for old-fashioned ice-cream floats and ice-cream sodas.

There's also an active grill here, perhaps best known for its ten-inch split-and-grilled hot dogs and for its quarter-pound single and double hamburgers and cheeseburgers. For a few extra coins, you can top any of these bad boys off with your choice of chili, grilled or raw onions, grilled peppers or mushrooms, bacon, sauerkraut, lettuce, or tomato.

Back to the deep fryers: The Blaneys' oil of choice is soy, and it's been trans-fat-free for the past eight years. The oil in the fryers is checked frequently and strained or replaced on a daily basis. So much of a clam shack's success rides on having clean oil, and the Blaneys are borderline fanatical about keeping theirs as clean and fresh as they can.

**THE** Sea Swirl sports classic roadside ice-cream-stand architecture.

Sea Swirl has a constantly rotating staff of fifteen or so young people helping out behind the counter and in the kitchen, all dressed in bright blue Sea Swirl T-shirts. Some are local college kids, and others come via work-study programs from such faraway places as Thailand, eastern Europe, and Zambia. The Blaneys' two daughters worked at Sea Swirl through their high-school years, and although they're both in their thirties and have moved on, they still pinch-hit from time to time when help is needed.

## Living on Red Sox Time

Let it be known that Sea Swirl serves baseball fans of all persuasions, but this is definitely a Red Sox shack all the way. It used to be that the Blaneys opened Sea Swirl on the Red Sox opening day and closed it when the season ended for their Boston heroes. In recent World Series years, this meant staying open throughout October and into November. Although Dave and Kathleen no longer run their shack on Red Sox time, they're still die-hard fans who follow the team's ups and downs year in and year out.

## MARKET NATIONALLY, SELL LOCALLY

Although Sea Swirl has, through its well-deserved media exposure over the years, developed a strong national reputation (and it boasts an enviable location in a highly trafficked tourist town), most of its customer base remains the loyal locals who keep coming back on a regular basis throughout the summer. The Blaneys have formed lasting friendships with many of these clam lovers (especially the Red Sox fans), and their business has benefited as a result. They also pull quite heavily from the Boston area; the baseball allegiance certainly hasn't hurt in that regard.

Yet it's the visitors from far-flung places who often make the biggest splash with the Blaneys. Many of these non–New England wayfarers have never seen, let alone tasted, a deep-fried whole-belly clam. It's as unusual and exotic to them as a rare French truffle or Amazonian orchid. Dave claims that about one in ten such visitors has his or her picture taken in front of the Sea Swirl sign while dangling a deep-fried whole-belly clam between pinched finger and thumb as proof that they've been to the mecca of fried clams in Mystic. Who can blame them for their excitement and their wonder?

# The Cove Clam Shack

20 Old Stonington Road, Mystic, CT 06378 | (860) 536-0061 | www.covefishmarket.com | Open year-round

**J**ust up the road from Sea Swirl on Route 1 as you head north toward Stonington, Connecticut, you'll notice on the left-hand side of the road what appears to be the bow portion of a beached and weather-beaten commercial fishing boat with cryptic advertising painted on some boards hanging off of it. OPEN 7 DAYS, INDOOR SEATING, OPEN ALL YEAR, and DAILY SPECIALS beckon you to turn left down Old Stonington Road to see what all the fuss is about. Well, it's about the Cove Clam Shack, a well-kept secret tucked away behind the old half-boat and a grove of trees—a combination clam shack and seafood market that may be hard to find but tough to beat.

Just like its boat-billboard by the highway, the Cove has a weathered look and feel to it. The seafood market and shack are housed side by side in a light-blue, one-story framed wooden structure. There are a couple of good-sized dining tents in front of the Cove, right next to the parking area. Each tent covers several picnic tables, providing shelter from sun and rain. There are also a bunch of tree-shaded, open-air picnic tables strung along the far side of the building for those interested in more secluded, open-air dining.

Don't be put off by the well-worn look of the place. What the Cove may seem to lack in snappiness it more than makes up for in character and fine food. A small amount of indoor seating was added to the seafood market area in 2005, and owner Andrew Kowal likes to think of the Cove as a "restaurant disguised as a clam shack." Some of the finer fare on the menu bears him out. But first, let's visit the take-out window, where the shack tradition lives on.

**A** sunny day at the Cove Clam Shack.

## AN *ESQUIRE* MAGAZINE TOP-25

The most popular thing to do at the Cove is to order up a bunch of deep-fried seafood from the take-out window on the right-hand side of the building and grab a seat at one of the picnic tables outside. There's a fairly wide variety of chowders, sandwiches, rolls, plates, and side orders to choose from, but the signature dish here is simply known as the Fish Sandwich. Now, before you roll your eyes in disbelief at such a pedestrian specialty, consider these accolades that have been bestowed on the Cove's signature sandwich:

**THE** Cove's award-winning fish sandwich.

- *Esquire* named it one of the top 25 sandwiches in the country in 2008.
- *Connecticut* magazine declared it to be the best sandwich in the state in 2008 and 2009.

These honors aren't just for fish sandwiches; they're for *any* type of sandwich. The Cove's winner consists of a very lightly breaded fillet of cod served with romaine lettuce and tomato slices on a simple, soft roll with tartar sauce on the side. It may not sound like much, but when you bite into the moist, tender cod and experience the heavenly mild flavor of the fresh fish, you'll understand what all the fuss is about. This sandwich alone is worth a special trip to the Cove.

The other item for which the Cove is best known is the Creamy Clam Chowder. This heady broth is thick with clams and potatoes and nicely seasoned with dill and other spices. There are two other things that Kowal says make his chowder a standout. The first is the fatback he uses in place of the more common salt pork when preparing his base for the chowder. The second is the vintage, inch-thick, galvanized aluminum pot he uses every day to prepare it. Whatever it is that makes it special, this chowder is a must-have, even if you don't plan to stick around for a meal.

# The Cove Spicy Fresh Fish Stew

Cove owner Andrew Kowal came up with this winning recipe himself, and he has a dedicated following of customers who come in regularly just for the stew. Give it a try and see what you think. (Andrew recommends cooking up a banquet-size vat of the stew so that you may freeze up a bunch for later eating, but feel free to reduce all the ingredients proportionately to fit your particular needs.)

INGREDIENTS

- 7 tablespoons good-quality olive oil
- 4½ cups chopped sweet onion
- 1½ pounds chopped green bell pepper
- 1½ teaspoons crushed red pepper flakes
- 3½ tablespoons minced garlic cloves
- 4½ pounds cut-up small red bliss potatoes, skin on
- 3 cans (28 ounces each) whole peeled San Marzano tomatoes, crushed
- 5 bay leaves
- ¾ gallon clam juice
- 3 cups chardonnay wine
- ½ can tomato paste
- Salt and pepper to taste
- Cod, raw shrimp, or mussels

### The Stock

This may be prepared in advance. Heat the olive oil in a very large, heavy pot over medium heat and sauté the onion, green pepper, crushed red pepper flakes, and garlic for five minutes. Add the potatoes, San Marzano tomatoes, bay leaves, clam juice, chardonnay, and tomato paste. Bring to a boil. Add salt and pepper to taste. Reduce to a simmer for 15 minutes or until the potatoes are done.

### The Seafood

Reheat the stock to near boiling, add generous portions of cod, raw shrimp, or mussels (or any combination of the three) and heat until the seafood is cooked through and tender.

Ladle the stew into a warm soup bowl, garnish with parsley, and serve with a side of grilled garlic bread. Refrigerate or freeze any excess stock for more stew at a later date.

## A Little Bit of History

The Cove began as just a seafood market stand owned by a fellow named Paul Barber back in 1964. A few years after opening, Barber started cooking up fish and chips on the side for his customers. As time rolled on, the menu grew to include fried clams, scallops, oysters, and shrimp and the aforementioned Creamy Clam Chowder, which Barber invented himself.

Much of the seafood for the market and the burgeoning clam shack came from the nearby town and port of Stonington, which until recently had a very active commercial fishing fleet. (It still has one, but not nearly as big as it was in its heyday.) Andrew says he now gets most of his seafood for both market and shack from New Bedford, Massachusetts, which has one of the largest and best commercial fishing operations in the country.

Andrew bought the business in 2003 and began running it pretty much as Barber had run it up until that point. In 2005, however, Kowal decided to add beer and wine to his offerings, and in order to do so, he had to enlarge his small seafood market area, install some indoor seating, and make other improvements to the property to be in compliance with local codes. Today the Cove is one of those somewhat rare shacks that offer beer and wine (by the glass or by the bottle) to customers. The wine list is short but quite nice, and the prices are very reasonable. You may still BYO, but there will be a corkage fee if you do.

**A** couple enjoying their repast in the Cove's shaded picnic area.

## A BIT OF EXOTICA

Andrew's son Zachary helped manage the business for five years before embarking on a career in music. Kowal then hired a manager who suggested putting grilled mahi mahi on the menu. Andrew was dubious but went along with it on a trial basis. It turned out to be a success with customers, and it has joined a growing number of grilled fish items. Another exotic item on the menu is the Cove Spicy Fresh Fish Stew (see sidebar for recipe), an alluring one-bowl meal made with fresh chunks of fish and shellfish, all simmered together in a broth that is made with San Marzano tomatoes imported from Italy, lots of vegetables, clam juice, and a good dose of chardonnay.

With the indoor seating, the wine list, and the sometimes fancy cookery, the Cove may appear to be more like a seafood restaurant and less like a shack, but when you pull in front and gape at the shabby-chic exterior, you'll know you're in shack territory—and you'll be glad that you are.

# Seafood Haven

668 Atlantic Avenue, Misquamicut, RI 02891 | (401) 322-0330 | Open April to mid-October

The Watch Hill and Misquamicut state beaches in southwestern Rhode Island attract thousands of sun-and-sand worshippers, mostly from nearby Connecticut, on sunny summer days. The vast stretches of open beach are a playground for young and old alike. The body surfing at high tide is excellent, and the people-watching all day long is even better.

With so many beachgoers pouring into the area for fun in the sun, there's plenty of demand for deep-fried seafood and other seaside snacks, and Seafood Haven fills that niche very nicely. Located about two miles east of Misquamicut State Beach on Atlantic Avenue, just before the Weekapaug Breachway, Seafood Haven's unassuming two-story frame exterior is easy to miss if you're not looking carefully for the roadside sign. Pull into the lot, and you'll notice right away that it's a bit of a schizophrenic operation: You have a choice between seafood takeout from the left-hand side of the building

**SEAFOOD** Haven, ready for business.

or pizza and grinders (a recent addition) on the right-hand side. Forget for now the pizza and grinders—we're here for seafood!

## A NOD TO THE NUTMEG STATE . . .

You may be wondering why this place is included with the Long Island Sound clam shacks to the west and south of Misquamicut when clearly the beach faces not the Sound but the open ocean. Geographically we're a bit off, but culturally and cuisine-wise we're in the right place because the vast majority of people visiting the area come from Connecticut, and they like their shack fare prepared in the style to which they're accustomed.

Seafood Haven owner Bob Barber started his career in the 1960s working with the Howard Johnson's chain of restaurants when it was in its heyday. HoJo's is famous for, among other things, taking the once quaintly regional clam strip and making it a national sensation. Bob toiled for the Blue and

Orange for a number of years before going to work for the Cozy Corner restaurant in Charlestown, Rhode Island. He eventually became owner of the Misquamicut seafood retailer Market by the Sea in 1993, and he changed the name to Seafood Haven shortly thereafter.

Before the recent arrival of pizza and grinders at the Haven, the other half of this shack was a combination snack bar and seafood market. Bob and his business partner, Caswell Cooke Jr., have seen the ups and downs of the local seafood scene over the past couple of decades, and they've carved out a solid reputation as the best place for fried clams and other seafood along Misquamicut's main drag.

SEAFOOD Haven's road sign reflects the dual nature of the establishment.

## . . . BUT STILL SOLIDLY IN RHODE ISLAND

Despite Seafood Haven's close cultural ties to Connecticut to the west, some things at the shack are Rhode Island through and through. For instance, its signature and perhaps most popular food item is its clam fritters (a Rhode

Island specialty), prepared fresh daily and fried in oil that's cleaned and replaced at least once a day. In fact, there's an entire deep fryer dedicated just to cooking up the fritters in Seafood Haven's small, bustling kitchen. A plate of fritters and a bowl of chowder make a fine meal, especially if you're looking for an alternative to the hefty deep-fried seafood platters on the rest of the menu.

So, after a day of riding the surf and soaking up the rays (don't forget the sunscreen!) at Misquamicut or Watch Hill, be sure to stop by Seafood Haven for a quick deep-fried seafood fix before heading back home.

# Johnny Angel's Clam Shack

**523 Charlestown Beach Road, Charlestown, RI 02813 | (401) 419-6732 (owner's cell phone number—call him, he doesn't mind!) | Open late May to early October**

If you happen to be cruising Route 1 in southern Rhode Island between Westerly and Narragansett, there's a nice detour down a series of quiet roads heading toward Charlestown beach that will take you right by a delightful little shack known as Johnny Angel's. Johnny's is a pleasant surprise for those lucky enough to stumble upon it or for anyone who takes the time to track it down.

This bona fide clam shack is situated between Ninigret and Green Hill Ponds, just a short distance from Charlestown's public beach. Johnny's shares its low-key, pond-side lot with a small marina and a kayak rental shop. The shack itself is a nondescript, single-room, white-washed building with a couple of screened order windows in front and a plain-looking railed-in deck extending off the back—but there's nothing ordinary about this nice little spot.

Owned and managed by the energetic, talkative, multitasking John Martin (he is, of course, the "Johnny" of Johnny Angel's), this delightful little eatery is a definite find for lovers of fried clams and other basic clam shack fare. John has had a lease on this place for the past ten years,

and he migrates to the shack each spring after working winters at one restaurant or another in Providence or Boston. He has an encyclopedic knowledge of the regional restaurant scenes in Rhode Island and eastern Massachusetts, right down to the financials of dozens of restaurants.

The shack is an old beach cottage that was relocated to its present site in the 1950s and then converted into a food stand. Although it sits in the midst of what is now a mostly residential beach community, it's been grandfathered into the neighborhood and is a favorite of local residents, beach house renters, and Charlestown beachgoers.

**JOHNNY** Angel's simple yet inviting sign.

## CLASSIC SHACK FARE

The menu at Johnny Angel's is simple and satisfying. A top choice is the fried whole-belly clams. Martin fries them up himself in his small, dimly lit kitchen behind the order windows. They're put through a wash, then lightly battered and fried to a golden brown, coming out crispy, crunchy, flavorful, and sweet. John's other standout item is his clam chowder, made fresh at least once a day in a huge stove-top chowder pot. Although Johnny Angel's is on the coast of southern Rhode Island, Martin's culinary roots lie mostly in the Providence and Boston areas, so he's concocted a thick, rich, and spicy New England–style chowder that goes great with his fried-to-order clam fritters. Both are chock-full of flavorful minced clams. Watching Martin move deftly around his compact kitchen, frying and grilling and ladling up his specialties, is an inspiration for anyone who has dreamed of opening a little eatery and having tons of fun running it.

Clam strips, fried scallops, and fish and chips round out the seafood offerings on Johnny's menu. For landlubbers, there are burgers, hot dogs, corn dogs, and a grilled chicken sandwich. Nibbling foods include fries, onion rings, chicken fingers, and mozzarella sticks. And that's about it—except for ice cream. Johnny's offers anywhere from six to ten different flavors at a time, and you may get large or small orders in a cup or a cone.

**JOHN** Martin, owner of Johnny Angel's Clam Shack.

**AN** order of whole-belly clams getting ready for the deep fryer.

## A Little Bit of Italy

Wednesday nights are pasta nights at Johnny Angel's—perhaps a nod to Rhode Island's large Italian-American population. Locals and house renters love to stop in with their own bottles of wine (it's BYO), sit on the deck, and converse while enjoying heaping plates of spaghetti, garlic bread, and salad.

### DON'T MISS THE SUNSETS

Because this place is nestled in among summer homes with few commercial enterprises in the area, it's got a loyal and somewhat captive following in the surrounding neighborhood. In addition, Charlestown residents stop by frequently on their way to and from the nearby town beach. There aren't a lot of customers from beyond the local area. So, when you're sitting on the deck, enjoying your meal, you may find yourself pulled into one local discussion or another, as if you were sitting out in a neighbor's backyard. It's a nice way to spend a sunny afternoon or evening, chatting with friendly strangers who make you feel right at home in their fun little corner of coastal Rhode Island.

One of the best times to be at Johnny Angel's is at sunset. The deck faces west toward Ninigret Pond, and couples and families congregate here to toast the end of the day and to watch the sun go down. It's also a great time to rent a kayak from the outfitter next door and take a paddle around the broad, shallow pond, which connects via a winding channel (known locally as a breachway) with the ocean nearby.

John Martin has a good thing going down here by the water in Charlestown. Let's hope the angels keep a watchful eye on this spot so that lovers of clams and beautiful sunsets will have an oasis here for many years to come.

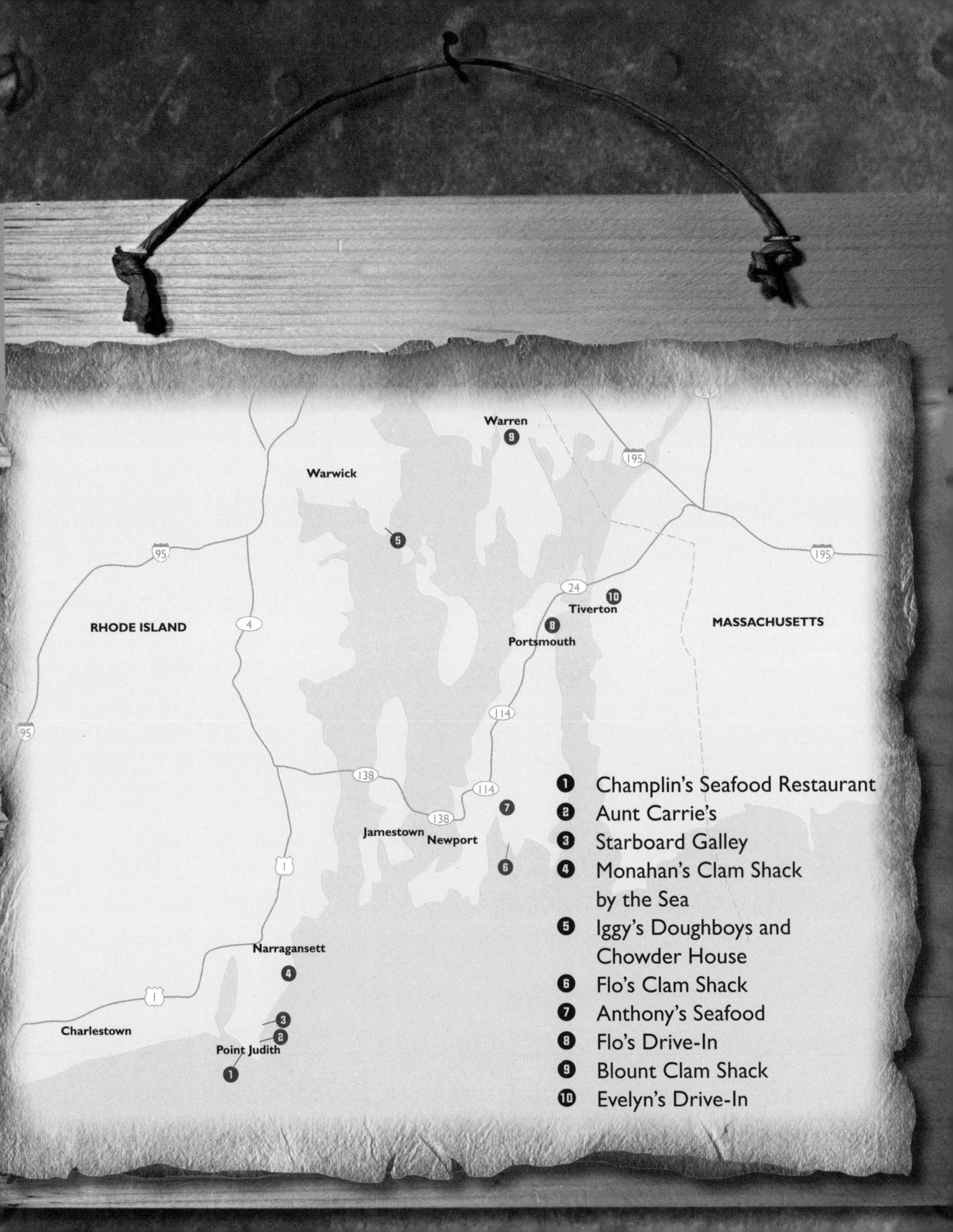

Warren

9

Warwick

195

5

95

24

10

Tiverton

8

RHODE ISLAND

4

Portsmouth

MASSACHUSETTS

195

114

95

138

114

1. Champlin's Seafood Restaurant
2. Aunt Carrie's
3. Starboard Galley
4. Monahan's Clam Shack by the Sea
5. Iggy's Doughboys and Chowder House
6. Flo's Clam Shack
7. Anthony's Seafood
8. Flo's Drive-In
9. Blount Clam Shack
10. Evelyn's Drive-In

138

7

Jamestown   Newport

6

1

Narragansett

4

1

3

Charlestown

2

Point Judith

1

# NARRAGANSETT BAY SHACKS

**T**he heart and soul of Rhode Island's nautical past and present may be found around Narragansett Bay, a large, island-strewn body of water that is New England's largest estuary. The bay's cities and towns, which include Providence, Newport, Narragansett, Barrington, and Jamestown, are home to the vast majority of the state's population—and virtually all of the region's clam shacks!

There are two concentrations of shacks around Narragansett Bay. The first includes the towns of Point Judith, Galilee, and Narragansett, clustered around the bay's southwestern corner, where there are popular state beaches and the ferry terminal for nearby Block Island. Thousands of people mob this area daily during the summer season, especially on weekends, and there are several fine clam shacks to choose from.

The other concentration of Narragansett Bay shacks is located on the bay's eastern shores from south of Providence down to Newport. This area tends to be the quieter, more laid-back part of Narragansett Bay (except for bustling Newport), and you will find some very nice, scenic clam shacks in this less traveled part of Rhode Island.

So, whether you crave the crowded scene at the beach or the tranquility of a back-road ramble, you may experience both in a relatively compact geographical area when you explore the shores and shacks of Narragansett Bay.

# Champlin's Seafood Restaurant

256 Great Island Road, Galilee, RI 02882 | (401) 783-3152 | www.champlins.com | Open year-round

Champlin's is a clam shack and so much more. In fact, in some ways it resembles an amusement park of seafood fun. You can wander from room to room and floor to floor in this sprawling dockside complex and really get a feel for the unique and important role that seafood plays in the culture and economy of this cheerful, bustling corner of Narragansett Bay.

## FRESH OFF THE BOAT

Let's start with the fish market on the first floor. It's basically your old-fashioned waterfront setup, with a poured concrete floor, a couple of large cold-water lobster tanks burbling away, and a modest glass-front counter displaying the day's catch in all its super-fresh glory. There are also a few tables along the walls, each covered with chipped ice and stacked with yet more fresh fish and shellfish. You can get a close-up look and literally pick out the items you want. The clam table is particularly alluring with its steamers, cherrystones, and littlenecks displayed in mounds of shells atop the ice and ready to be had, either steamed or raw.

Champlin's is also in the wholesale seafood business, and their dockside location serves them well. They've got their own wood-shingled receiving shed on their dock in back of the building. Each day starting at 6 a.m., commercial fishing and lobster boats tie up and offload their

**CHAMPLIN'S** offers a wide variety of seafood fun.

## Some Lobster Facts

Here are some facts about everyone's favorite red crustacean, courtesy of the folks at Champlin's, who catch and sell thousands of lobsters every year:

✪ A lobster takes eighteen to twenty-four months to develop from the time of impregnation to the hatching of the egg.

✪ A lobster is the size of a mosquito when it leaves the female's body.

✪ As a lobster grows, it sheds its shell, increasing in weight by 25 percent each time.

✪ A lobster will shed its shell twenty-four times in the first year of life.

✪ An older lobster only molts once every four or five years.

✪ A lobster is approximately seven years old before it's legal to harvest. It will weigh approximately one pound at that time.

✪ A lobster's age in years may be determined by taking its weight in pounds, multiplying it by four, then adding three.

✪ A lobster that has lost a claw is called a "cull." The lost claw will regenerate.

✪ A lobster with no claws is called a "bullet."

catches into Champlin's waiting coolers and tanks. The dropoffs continue throughout the day, so you're guaranteed the freshest of fish both in the seafood market and in the restaurant upstairs.

## LET'S EAT!

Going back outside, there are a couple of staircases leading to the second floor of the building, which consists of a food-ordering window, a small service bar, and several indoor and outdoor dining areas. Be prepared: On busy summer days, there is often a line of customers winding down the stairs and out into the street, waiting to place their orders. Peak waiting time to place your order on the busiest days in July and August can be up to forty minutes.

Be assured, however, that it's well worth the wait. Champlin's is famous throughout the region for its dry-batter fried seafood as well as its steamed lobsters and clams, lobster rolls, chowders, and clam cakes. Their kitchen is a paragon of efficiency, and they keep the line of customers moving quickly.

While you're waiting, you should snag a paper menu and peruse the offerings so that you're ready to order when you reach the front of the line. The small flier is full of helpful information on various dishes and the options for side orders with each dinner. This little cheat sheet will most likely answer all of your questions before you arrive at the order window, saving you and everyone else precious time between anticipation and indulgence.

## WHAT TO ORDER

Co-owner Brian Handrigan is rightfully proud of the fried whole-belly clams that are the signature dish at Champlin's. These small, sweet, tender morsels are lightly breaded and flash-fried in soybean oil so they don't get overcooked. The clam strips, with their distinctive hard-shell clam flavor, are similarly prepared and served in copious amounts as part of a dinner platter that includes french fries or red potatoes and coleslaw.

Flounder is the fried fish of choice at Champlin's—a thin fillet that's breaded, very fresh, and sweet in flavor. You may have this as a dinner, in a delightful sandwich, or as the centerpiece of Champlin's overwhelming Seafood Platter. It's one of the nicest pieces of fried fish you'll find anywhere.

The sea scallops come from local scallop boats that drop off their catch at Champlin's dock daily. They have a unique smoky, almost grilled flavor and are lightly seasoned with a paprika-like spice. The gulf shrimp are plump, juicy, and particularly good with Champlin's homemade cocktail sauce.

Chowders here are extremely popular, and Champlin's sticks close to the Rhode Island style for each one. Several large vats of clear-broth chowder are cooked up on the kitchen's stove top daily and served in three varieties: red (with a little bit of fresh tomato mixed in), white (with a splash of milk, not cream), and the straight-up clear-broth variety. Try a bowl accompanied by Champlin's sweet, puffy clam cakes, another local favorite.

A lot of steamed lobster is sold at Champlin's in the summer, and you have the option of going downstairs to the seafood market and picking out which one you want. They'll snag it out of the tank, take it upstairs, and steam it up for you either to enjoy on the premises or to take home. Red potatoes and corn on the cob make excellent side dishes.

## WHERE TO EAT

After surviving the line, placing your order, and scoring your cafeteria tray full of food, you have several choices of where to enjoy your repast. The most popular (and probably the most fun) place is out on the second floor covered deck just outside the order/pickup area. There are some twenty picnic-style tables under a large blue awning that protects you from sun and rain.

In more blustery weather, Champlin's installs Plexiglas panels around the sides to keep out cold breezes and blowing rain. The deck has a great view of the fishing boats and docks and the channel through which the Block Island ferry passes numerous times each day. You're so close to the channel, it seems as if you can reach out and touch the ferry as it passes, and there's lots of good-natured waving between strangers from the deck of the restaurant and the deck of the boat.

If you'd rather stay indoors, there's a spacious, wood-paneled dining room just off the other side of the order/pickup area, filled with varnished wooden booths. The walls are covered with great historical photos of Champlin's over the years, surviving (more or less) several hurricanes and snow-storms and growing from a simple waterside market into the behemoth that it is today. If these spots don't suit you, then head back downstairs to the half-dozen or so picnic tables next to Champlin's waterside ice-cream stand, where cups, cones, sundaes, and fudge are served up in season. This is a good spot for those seeking the warmth of the sun and a great waterline view of the harbor.

## How *Do* They Get Here?

Parking can be a challenge when you're circling Champlin's, looking for a place to ditch your car. There are a mere twelve parking places in front and a limited amount of free spots in a shared lot across the street. You can always park just down the street in the massive lot for Block Island ferry passengers, but that will cost you the daily rate of approximately $10.

Champlin's owners Brian Handrigan and Bob Mitchell always marvel at the crowds outside their establishment in the summer, wondering where they park before queuing up. Surprisingly, few customers ever complain about the parking challenges, which seems to testify to the enduring reputation of Champlin's as a place that's definitely worth jumping through some hoops for. With a little bit of patience and hopefully some luck on the parking scene, you're pretty much guaranteed a memorable meal and dockside experience at Champlin's Seafood of Galilee.

**CHAMPLIN'S** bustling order and pickup windows are busy throughout the summer.

# Aunt Carrie's

1240 Ocean Road, Narragansett, RI 02882 | (401) 783-7930 | www.auntcarriesri.com
**Open April to late September**

The countdown has begun for the 100th anniversary of Aunt Carrie's Restaurant in Narragansett, Rhode Island. Originally opened in 1920 by Aunt Carrie Cooper, it has been owned and operated by the same family ever since. The Cooper family currently has third and fourth generation members in the business, and there's every reason to believe that the dynasty will continue well into the twenty-first century.

## INVENTORS OF THE CLAM CAKE?

Back in the early 1900s, Carrie Cooper and her husband Ulysses made regular trips with their children in their Model-T Ford from Connecticut to Narragansett for seaside camping vacations. They started selling lemonade to local fishermen and other campers to help subsidize their travels, and eventually Carrie started cooking up pots of clam chowder, which she made from the clams her children gathered along the beach.

Carrie thought it might be interesting to dice up some of the clams and blend them into her corn fritters, which she fried up at the campsite. The alluring aroma of these deep-fried delights wafted over to other campsites, attracting curious neighbors who found the fried cakes delicious. Carrie and Ulysses were inspired to open a small snack stand near the present location of the Point Judith lighthouse, where they started selling their clam cakes, chowder, and lemonade.

The couple eventually bought the land where the restaurant is currently located, and they erected the shingled shack that eventually became known as Aunt Carrie's. Much of the original structure still remains as the core of the current restaurant, with various minor additions and expansions tacked on over the

**AUNT** Carrie's looks much as it did when it opened decades ago.

years. Whether or not Carrie Cooper was the first person to make clam cakes in Rhode Island (or anywhere, for that matter), the fact remains that Aunt Carrie's has some of the best clam cakes to be found anywhere, and the Coopers have built their shack's reputation on them.

## A GREAT PLACE IN A GREAT SPOT

Located approximately halfway between Scarborough State Beach to the north and Point Judith (the port for the Block Island ferry) to the south, Aunt Carrie's is in the perfect spot to cater to beachgoers, boaters, anglers, and island hoppers all summer long. The building, little changed in outward appearance since it opened, has a delightful screened-in front porch with several tables facing the order and pickup counters for wonderfully breezy in-the-rough dining.

There is also a sit-down, full-service restaurant section that wraps around the side and the back of the building. In addition, there are a number of picnic tables and Adirondack chairs scattered around the grounds, most of them overlooking a lovely salt marsh. A short path at the edge of the marsh leads through some sand dunes to a nearby beach, in case you want to take a stroll by the surf. On busy summer days, the bulk of Aunt Carrie's customer traffic flows through the front-counter area for in-the-rough dining and carryout service, clearly the preferred way to enjoy a meal here.

## AUNT CARRIE'S FAMOUS SHORE DINNERS

Although there is plenty of wonderful fried seafood to be had at Carrie's (especially the whole-belly clams and the locally harvested flounder), the big deal here is the Rhode Island Shore

Dinner in any of its variant forms. These complete meals are the perfect way to cap off a day at the beach or a week on the Block. The dinners start with a bowl of Carrie's chowder (take your pick between what they refer to as milk, tomato, or plain—translated: New England,

## Aunt Carrie's Now Sells Ice Cream

Aunt Carrie's recently opened an ice-cream stand directly across the street from the clam shack. Sheathed in the same wood-shingle finish as Aunt Carrie's, the ice-cream annex offers an amazing variety of frozen treats. There are more than forty flavors of ice cream to choose from, all of them homemade from the Ice Cream Machine of Cumberland, Rhode Island.

Try one of their creative sundaes, such as the Rhody, the Beach Bonfire, the Block Island Surprise, the Dirty Fisherman, and others. Homemade pie frappes are available in apple, banana, and key lime flavors. Del's Frozen Lemonade is another favorite at the stand, in case you prefer something more on the thirst-quenching side. In addition, there's a cute little gift shop on the east end of the building where you may purchase Aunt Carrie's, Block Island, and Rhode Island memorabilia in the form of T-shirts, postcards, books, and more.

Manhattan, or Rhode Island). The chowder is accompanied by four fluffy clam cakes. Next is a generous portion of steamed clams with melted butter, followed by a tasty fish-and-chips platter.

Don't think that'll be enough? You can add a 1¼-pound lobster to your shore dinner, if you like. And be sure to save room for one of Aunt Carrie's homemade desserts, which comes as part of the shore dinner package. The Cooper family bakes up a storm in their kitchen, and there are always fresh pies, puddings, shortcakes, and loaves of bread available to enjoy with your meal or (in the case of whole pies and loaves of bread) to take home. Mini Shore Dinners are available for those not quite up for the entire thing. Whether you decide to go for the whole shebang or the more modest Mini Shore, either way you're in for a major Rhode Island seafood feast!

Although Iggy's Doughboys and Chowderhouse of Warwick has opened up a carryout clam shack kitty-corner to Aunt Carrie's, it doesn't appear to have put much of a dent in Carrie's thriving business, a testament to the loyal legions of customers who have come to Carrie's for generations and will most likely continue to do so for as long as the Cooper family keeps its doors open.

# Starboard Galley

**5 Angell Road, Narragansett, RI 02882 | (401) 782-1366 | www.starboardgalleyrestaurant.com**
**Open June to mid-October**

This shack might best be nicknamed "The Wanderer." Having changed locations twice in the past several years, Starboard Galley still has a loyal following, and as they say themselves, they serve the "Best Chowda and Clamcakes Anywhere!"

Owners Molly Marks and Tom Silvia are passionate about the seafood business, having been partners in one gustatory enterprise or another over the past twenty-five years. Tom was also a commercial lobsterman for twenty years, and he knows how to procure the best fresh fish and shellfish in this corner of Narragansett Bay. Molly is the day-to-day operator of Starboard Galley, handling the service counter and dining area. In addition to her boundless energy and her gift for gab, she has brought her grandmother's signature chowder recipe to Starboard Galley. (Don't even bother to ask if she'll share it. The recipe's too good to give away.)

**STARBOARD** Galley stakes its reputation on its tasty clam cakes and clam chowder.

## A Little Bit of History

Starboard Galley has been in three different locations in the past fifteen years. It first opened on the south end of Narragansett's seawall in 1996 and served up seafood and sandwiches from that location for the next ten years. When their lease came up for renewal, Molly and Tom decided to make a big move down to Charlestown, some fifteen miles to the south and west, to a spot near Rhode Island's scenic shoreline on the Atlantic Ocean. The Charlestown location featured an edgy dining area designed by Molly and Tom, with lots of locally produced art on the walls, stained glass, and tile-topped tables and counters. Molly has a background in theater, and live entertainment and performances were part of the mix at the Charlestown location.

After a few years, it became apparent that the new spot in Charlestown was a wee bit quiet to sustain the business. So, in

2010 it was back to Narragansett, this time to a converted, L-shaped pizza-restaurant building directly across from Scarborough Beach, a summertime hotspot in the Narragansett/Point Judith area. Much of the cool artwork and stained glass came along, as well as the sign bearing Starboard Galley's battle cry, no matter where they are: THE BEST CHOWDA AND CLAM-CAKES ANYWHERE!

## CHOWDA AND CLAM CAKES AND MORE

On to the clam cakes! These tasty morsels are truly unique and somewhat addictive, as they are lighter and fluffier than most you'll encounter elsewhere, and they're seasoned in a way that's both subtle and distinctive. Like any good snack food, it's not possible to have just one. Molly says that, during the busy summer months, a line forms outside the take-out window about thirty minutes before the 11 a.m. opening time—they're all there for their clam-cake "brunch," and Molly, Tom, and their bustling staff are only too happy to oblige.

The secret-recipe clam chowder is a hybrid of sorts—lightly thickened à la New England, tomatoey à la Manhattan and Rhode Island red, and well seasoned for a distinctive flavor. Molly thickens her chowder naturally, using lots of potatoes that are expertly cooked down so that they blend in seamlessly with the broth. The chowder serves as an excellent complement to the clam cakes, which are perfect for dunking.

Due to popular demand, pizza has remained on the menu at the new locale, but it's the seafood that keeps 'em coming back. Of particular note are the various seafood sandwich rolls, beginning with the lobster rolls. You may have it one of two ways at Starboard Galley: there's a cold salad roll and what they call a "sauté roll," which is served warm with butter. Both are heaped with fresh-picked lobster meat and served on a toasted split-top bun. Other rolls include fried clam, clam strips, scallops, shrimp, tuna, seafood, or a spicy crabmeat chipotle roll.

The fried clams are nicely done here, both the whole bellies and the strips, and they may be had à la carte or as dinner plates with french fries and homemade coleslaw. Other fried dinner plates include fish and chips (with flounder), clam strips, shrimp, scallops, calamari, lobster, and the all-encompassing Fisherman's Platter. There's a nice daily special that's appropriate for lunch or dinner: an English-style fish and chips with one flounder fillet, fries, a cup of chowder, and two clam cakes at a very affordable price. This mini platter gives you the best of what Starboard Galley has to offer. Don't pass it up!

# Monahan's Clam Shack by the Sea

**190 Ocean Road, Narragansett, RI 02882 | (401) 782-2524 | www.monahansri.com**
**Open mid-May to early September**

There's a little shack with a lot of history at the south end of Narragansett's famed seawall, and it's a great place to stop for a snack or a meal if you happen to be in the area for a swim or a stroll or on vacation by the bay.

Monahan's Clam Shack has been around in one form or another on and off (mostly on) for the past several decades. It's currently owned and operated by Matt Combs, his sister Bridgett, and their brother Clayton, who are the third generation of a local family to serve up deep-fried fare in this scenic stand by the bay.

## A Family Affair

Joseph Monahan, the Combs's grandfather, originally got things going on this spot with a gas station and snack stand that eventually morphed into a clam shack and dairy bar in order to cater to beachgoers and summer vacationers in the area. Joseph eventually turned the business over to his son Michael (the Combs's uncle), who carried on the clam shack tradition for a number of years before passing away about a dozen years ago.

Matt, who was living in South Carolina at the time, had little interest in taking over the business, so the family leased the spot to Tom Silvia and Molly Marks, current owners of the nearby Starboard Galley. Tom and Molly sold their clam cakes and chowda, along with fried seafood, from the spot for several years before relocating their eatery to Charlestown.

When the shack perched on the seawall once again became available around 2006, Matt and his siblings decided to relaunch Monahan's and

**MONAHAN'S** is a cute little shack with a side patio overlooking Narragansett Bay.

give the fried seafood business a try, making them the third generation in the extended Monahan family to run the place. They haven't regretted it. Each year their business has increased, and they have plans to expand and upgrade Monahan's to accommodate the expected increase in business in the years to come.

## "Clam Cakes and Chowda"

Whether it's been Monahan's or Starboard Galley at any given time, clam cakes and chowder have always been mainstays of this sturdy little operation. They're the most popular items on the Monahan's menu, with hundreds of orders logged daily during the busy summer season. The clam cakes are light and fluffy, and the chowder comes in three tasty varieties: white (New England), red (Manhattan), and broth (Rhode Island). Despite Monahan's location in the (clear broth) Ocean State, Matt says that the creamy New England chowder is by far the most popular.

Also on the menu is a fine fish and chips dinner, featuring light and flaky locally caught flounder. The whole-belly clam dinner is also popular, as well as the scallops dinner and an unusual and tasty crab cake dinner. Lots of hamburgers, cheeseburgers, hot dogs, and grilled cheese sandwiches are also sold on hot summer days, as well as a hefty and rather pricey lobster salad roll. There's ice cream for dessert or snacking and smoothies for healthful refreshment, made fresh on the spot in Monahan's blenders.

## Sitting by the Dock on the Bay

Monahan's is blessed with a wonderful location, at the south end of Narragansett's seawall and also at the foot of a state pier where boats are launched and people congregate for lovely views up and down the shoreline. Matt installed a patio and awning next to the shack in 2010 to give his customers a catbird seat for gazing out on Narragansett Bay. It's a great place to enjoy the ocean breezes and to watch the multitude of foot traffic that passes by all day long. The patio also overlooks the pier and all its boat traffic.

Parking can sometimes be a challenge here. There are a few spots out front, and if you're lucky, you may be able to grab one along the seawall. In addition, there is public parking by the pier.

Don't despair. Even if you have to cruise the area for a little while in search of a place to park your car, you'll be amply rewarded with a nice meal in a beautiful spot at Monahan's Clam Shack by the Sea.

# Iggy's Doughboys & Chowder House

**889 Oakland Beach Avenue, Warwick, RI 02889 | (401) 737-9459 | www.iggysdoughboys.com**
**Open year-round**

Judging from the snappy-looking exterior of Iggy's Doughboys and Chowder House, you'd never guess that this building started out as one of the oldest beachside food stands in Rhode Island. Way back in 1924, a snack shack named Gus's opened here in Warwick's Oakland Beach neighborhood on Greenwich Bay, selling soda, doughboys, and roller-coaster tickets to locals who came to the amusement park at Oakland Beach. The building survived two hurricanes, and the amusement park is long gone; but there's still a stand here, and it's grown into a really nice one that serves up doughboys and soda along with an amazing variety of clam shack fare.

Iggy's started with a simple menu of clam cakes, clam chowder, and doughboys—simple snacks for locals who spent hot summer days at Oakland Beach right next to Iggy's. Over time the menu has grown to include award-winning fried clams and other seafood, the renowned Iggy Burger, lots of other fried and grilled dishes, and Iggy's own "homemade" soda, which comes in over half a dozen different flavors.

## LONG LINES, SWEET REWARDS

Iggy's is indeed an oasis of sorts on the edge of a middle-class, mostly residential neighborhood of modest frame houses occasionally separated by empty lots that are remnants of past hurricane destruction. Though Iggy's façade is brightly decorated with its big sign and its signature dancing doughboy, chances are you'll

### Who Is Iggy?

The short answer is: Gaetano Gravino, who used to work at Gus's snack stand and who eventually bought the business in 1989. At the time, Gaetano drove a car with the Rhode Island licence plate IG6. Gravino's son David thought it looked like "IGG," and he took to calling his father by that nickname. Gaetano was not amused.

When the Gravinos took ownership of Gus's in 1989, they brainstormed within the family for a new restaurant name, and Dave gamely suggested "Iggy's." Gaetano must have gotten over his objections because the name stuck and Iggy's was born.

notice the line of customers snaking along the street in front of Iggy's before you come upon the shack itself. This place is immensely popular, especially in the summertime, and long waits may be expected, especially during the peak lunch and dinner hours. Once you make your way to the window on the street and place your order, you may also want to purchase an "I Survived the Line at Iggy's" T-shirt while you wait for your number to be called.

The wait at Iggy's may seem daunting, but the food is well worth it. For starters, the clam cakes and chowder are excellent, especially the red Manhattan version of the chowder, which is the shack's original style. Both are on the creamy side, which makes dunking the light, fluffy clam cakes into your chowder all the more enjoyable.

The deep-fried clams are light and sweet and served by the pint or as part of a dinner that includes chowder or salad, french fries, and coleslaw. The fish and chips features north Atlantic cod and is also served with chowder or salad and slaw.

On the Italian side of things are shaved steak and cheese, sausage and pepper, and meatball sandwiches as well as chicken parmesan and eggplant parmesan sandwiches. Other fun items include a crispy fried fish sandwich and Iggy's stuffed quahogs, which make a fine appetizer or snack.

On the healthy side, you'll find several salads, including a particularly tasty one that has a generous portion of cold lobster mixed in. There's also

**RARE** is the occasion that you'll find such a short line at Iggy's order window beneath the smiling, dancing Doughboy.

Rhode Island's signature garlicky snail salad on the menu for those adventurous enough to give it a try.

## DINING OPTIONS

The best thing about dining at Iggy's is the amazing views of Oakland Beach and Greenwich Bay just south of the shack. The Gravinos added on an enclosed dining area to the south end of the building several years ago, which provides year-round seating at approximately fifteen booths and tables. In fair weather, the best place to go is out on the shaded patio, which faces the beach and provides great views and cool breezes. There are also some picnic tables a short walk away at the beach, should you wish to be even closer to the water.

## SAVE SOME ROOM FOR DOUGHBOYS!

In some circles, it's considered impolite to partake of dessert before the main course. With doughboys in hand, however, it's awfully hard to resist diving into these deep-fried, sugar-coated pillows of dough before you've finished your meal. Good luck trying to keep your young ones away from these tasty treats before they've had their lunch or dinner.

Iggy's doughboys are cooked to order in the deep fryer, and each batch is placed in a paper bag along with a couple of generous scoops of sugar. Tradition dictates that you shake your bag around to ensure a thorough coating of sugar on all the doughboys. It's not uncommon to see smiling customers walking down the street, shaking their freshly procured doughboy bags in preparation for the sugary treats within.

## FAMILY-FRIENDLY COUPONS

The Gravinos have carefully cultivated the family crowd at their shack, and they have an aggressive coupon campaign going at all times to lure families in for excellent food at bargain prices. Check out their website, where you can print out the latest coupon offerings, or simply wait until you get to Iggy's, where you'll find coupons included with the flyers and carryout menus at the order windows.

In case you can't make it to Warwick to enjoy a meal and some doughboys at Iggy's, there's another location in Narragansett that's open seasonally from March through Columbus Day. With these two locations, Iggy's pretty well has the western shores of Narragansett Bay covered. What's next?

# Flo's Clam Shack

**4 Wave Avenue, Middletown, RI 02842 | (401) 847-8141 | www.flosclamshack.net | Open March through Decemb**

**F**lo's Clam Shack, in Middletown, Rhode Island, is just east of bustling Newport, and as such, it tends to be a little more laid back and informal than many of Newport's fancier eateries. That's a good thing. Flo's is a really fun place—an expanded two-story beach cottage filled with all sorts of kitschy nautical décor, and it's right across the street from one of the area's most popular beaches. Plenty of beach bums make their way over to Flo's for deep-fried seafood and a cold beer or two on the shack's festive outdoor decks and picnic tables in the summertime.

If you arrive by car, keep in mind that parking is to be found in back of Flo's, so swing around the corner, look for the plain, red-lettered word CLAMS emblazoned on the back of the building, and pull into the shack's narrow parking lot. From there, you'll have a short, adventurous walk up a wooden ramp that's enshrouded in a thick forest of twenty-foot-high bamboo shoots and leaves. When you emerge, you'll find yourself at the order window, which greets you on the side of the building. There's often a line snaking back into the bamboo tunnel, but it moves quickly and it's a peaceful, shady place to wait your turn.

## GRAB A TABLE FIRST

Before you get in line to order, you're encouraged to stake out a table for you and your mates in one of Flo's numerous dining areas. There are a lot of options packed into a relatively small amount of space. You may opt for the picnic tables in front of the shack, sheltered from the street by lots of tall sea grass, or you may go inside for more options. The first floor features a dining room with varnished-wood tables and

**FLO'S** Clam Shack is two floors of deep-fried fun in the sun.

chairs and lots of nautical stuff hanging from the walls and ceiling. Going upstairs, there are more fishing nets and buoys to gawk at, open-air decks in front and on the side, a small enclosed dining room in the middle, and in the back a full-service liquor bar and a raw bar that features local oysters and clams as well as crab legs and boiled shrimp.

Although Flo's is perfectly fine for families, the liquor flows a bit more freely here than at many other clam shacks, giving the place a bit more of an adult atmosphere. This is not to say families aren't comfortable here; au contraire, plenty of them dine here regularly and repeatedly and with good reason. The food is great, the beach is nearby, and the atmosphere is always cheerful. Plus, if you want to have a cold one while dining on some fine seafood with your kids, you have that option.

## FOR STARTERS

Once your table is secured and you've made your way to the front of the line at the order window, it's decision-making time. Given the excellent starters that Flo's has to offer, you may only need to load up on them and come back a second time for their main dishes.

Flo's chowders are rich and flavorful and come in three varieties: Rhode Island red, a zesty tomato-based chowder; white, in the

### Flo's Rocks!

There's an unusual custom at Flo's that's as charming as it is surprising. When you're at the order window, you'll notice a plastic bucket on the counter containing a bunch of smooth rocks with numbers painted on them. These are the claim checks for food orders. Once you've placed your order and settled up (cash only), you'll be given a numbered rock, which is your only stake to claiming your food when it's ready. Don't lose that stone!

more traditional New England mode; and clear broth, the classic Rhode Island version of clam chowder. A bowl of any can be a meal in itself, so you may wish to opt for the cup-size version.

One must-have appetizer at Flo's is their famous stuffed quahog clam, commonly known throughout shackdom as a "stuffie." Flo's version is based on an "ancient Portuguese recipe," which means it packs a spicy kick. You get a generous scoop of breaded stuffing that's chock-full of clam meat and seasonings, and it's encased within two good-sized quahog clam shells, often held together with a thick rubber band. A couple of stuffies are another excellent way to kick things off.

If chowder and stuffies don't bang your gong,

then try the clam cakes. These deep-fried balls of dough, minced clam, and seasonings make a great complement for dunking into a cup or bowl of chowder. Flo's clam cakes fare well in comparison to others in the area; they're flavorful, a bit oily, and the soft breaded insides are chewy and sweet. Flo's claims to have sold more than thirty million clam cakes over the years, but half a dozen should do you just fine.

There's also a "Greek Salad Made by a Greek" (always an encouraging sign), and it's big enough to be a meal in itself. You may wish to share it with a dining companion before moving on to more serious fare.

## PLATTERS AND COMBOS

Flo's built its reputation on fried clams, and you may have them here in a variety of ways. First, there are the whole bellies, sweet and chewy, lightly breaded, and full of briny flavor. The clam strips are lighter in color, equally flavorful, chewy, and plentiful when ordered as a platter, which comes with french fries and coleslaw.

The fried fish fillets at Flo's are battered, not breaded, in keeping with the classic fish and chips style. The white, flaky haddock fillet initially has a crunchy texture when you bite into the battered coating, then the sweet flavor of the fish comes through—a very pleasant one-two punch.

Scallops are on the gargantuan side, and it usually takes more than one bite to enjoy each one. Calamari, oysters, and shrimp round out the offerings from the deep fryer, and all may be had separately or as part of the Fisherman's Platter, which contains a lot (not a little) of everything, along with fries and slaw.

Most of the deep-fried offerings may also be had on toasted buns as rolls, and there's an exceptional lobster roll served cold, with mayo on the side. The fish sandwich is very popular and a great way to try Flo's battered fillet without filling up on the side orders.

Flo's combos feature mostly burgers and hot dogs from the grill, and each comes with fries, slaw, and a choice of soda or Bud draft beer. All combos are more than reasonably priced and a good way to fill up any of your kids who may turn their noses up at the seafood offerings.

There's one combo that will certainly raise your eyebrows as you scan the menu: a bottle of Moët Champagne and two "gourmet" hot dogs for $50. What the . . . ? No one seems to know how this got started or how many are sold. And the "gourmet" sobriquet for the wieners is definitely tongue-in-cheek. If you think you're up to the audacious pairing of grilled pups and a bottle of bubbly, by all means plunk down your Ulysses S. Grant and have a ball!

# Flo's Drive-In: The Job of Clam Shacks

. . . as in the biblical Job. The original Flo's Drive-In is located about ten miles north of Flo's Clam Shack. It's in the town of Portsmouth, on the broad, tidal Sakonnet River, which forms the easternmost portion of Narragansett Bay. This little shack has suffered mightily over the years, and it has quite a story to tell:

Flo's Drive-In opened in the Island Beach section of Portsmouth in 1936, operating out of an old chicken coop relocated to the beachfront and retrofitted for the fried clam business. Two years later, the great New England hurricane of 1938 roared up the bay and destroyed the shack. A new one was built shortly thereafter to replace it.

Business picked up over the years, and then in 1954, Hurricane Carol inflicted heavy damage to Flo's. A new building was brought to the site. Six years later, Hurricane Donna smacked Flo's

and washed it up the road. Then, in 1991, Hurricane Bob scored a direct hit on Portsmouth, and once again Flo's was obliterated. When the waters receded after Bob, the only thing remaining was the Flo's Drive-In sign.

Amazingly, the shack was rebuilt, and the cedar-shingled shanty remains defiantly standing to this day—open seasonally yet always looking over its shoulder for the next big blow. There's a small, hand-painted sign on the side of Flo's Drive-In that simply declares CLOSED HURRICANES. Prescient.

As a hedge against further mayhem, owner Komes Rozes decided to open the companion Flo's Clam Shack in Middletown in 1992. It's housed in a sturdy, two-story beach cottage that survived the hurricanes that brought so much trouble to Flo's Drive-In. No big storms have threatened either shack since then. Long live both locations!

# Anthony's Seafood

963 Aquidneck Avenue, Middletown, RI 02842 | (401) 846-9620 | www.anthonysseafood.net | Open year-roun

Another fine seafood shack just outside of Newport is Anthony's Seafood, located about a mile north and east of Flo's on Aquidneck Avenue (Route 138). Anthony's is equal parts seafood market and clam shack with indoor and outdoor in-the-rough seating. It's set back from the road in a nondescript building on a commercial strip of Aquidneck Avenue, so it's easy to drive by and not notice it. Keep your eyes peeled because this place is definitely worth a stop.

When you first step inside Anthony's, it becomes immediately clear that the main business here is retail seafood, with its long, gleaming counter and amazing variety of fresh fish and shellfish atop crushed ice in glass cases that run nearly thirty feet from one end of the room to the other. However, don't overlook the two small dining rooms to the right of the cases. There's a cash register at the end of the seafood cases, and it is here that you may place your order for some of the best deep-fried, baked, and grilled seafood in greater Newport.

## A LITTLE HISTORY

Anthony's has a long and colorful history in the Newport seafood business, having begun as a wholesale lobster company on Spring Wharf on the Newport waterfront in 1956. Founder Anthony Bucolo eventually expanded into the wholesale fish business, and boats were soon bringing fresh catches daily from Gloucester and New Bedford, Massachusetts, and from points as far south as North Carolina.

Bucolo added a retail seafood business in 1972 and a floating dockside restaurant in 1980. Anthony and his sons sold the business in the

**HUNGRY** customers gather around the order counter at Anthony's.

mid-1980s but bought it back a few years later when it fell on hard times and moved it to its present location in 1989. The focus over the past twenty years has shifted from seafood wholesaling to preparing and selling the finest fresh seafood for walk-in customers throughout the Newport area.

**ANTHONY'S** offers alfresco dining in front of its low-key Aquidneck Avenue building.

## NEWPORT SEAFOOD AT ITS FINEST

There's usually a small crowd of people milling around the cash register, studying oversized laminated menus, which may be picked up at a small kiosk across from the register. Grab one and feast your eyes on the many different seafood snacks and meals that Anthony's produces in its relatively small kitchen.

The best starters are the spicy Portuguese fish chowder, chock-full of fish and shellfish and flavored with chouriço; the Kung Pao calamari, served with hot peppers, plum sauce, peanuts, and scallions; and the stuffies (stuffed Quahog clams), spiced with chouriço as well as onions and peppers and served either hot or mild.

As for main courses, try the fish taco sandwich, a burrito-like flour tortilla stuffed with fried flounder, lettuce, tomato, black beans, and cheese. The fried calamari dinner is renowned and perhaps the best of the offerings among the many deep-fried seafood platters. The steamers come in meal-sized portions (two pounds), accompanied by both butter and broth. Among the baked dinners, go for the baked stuffed sole, two fillets packed with seafood stuffing and topped with a creamy lobster sauce.

Though Anthony's may have surrendered its precious dockside location in downtown Newport twenty-plus years ago, the Bucolos have no regrets and neither do their customers, many of whom are loyal locals. (It's always a good idea to go where the locals go.) What Anthony's may have sacrificed in terms of a scenic, bustling downtown location they've more than made up for with excellent seafood served in a casual, out-of-the-way, in-the-rough dining atmosphere. Check 'em out.

# Blount Clam Shack

335 Water Street, Warren, RI 02885 | (401) 245-3210 | www.blountseafood.com/clam-shack
Open May to early September

Blount Clam Shack is definitely one of the more pleasant surprises in scenic eastern Rhode Island—and that's saying a lot because there are plenty of wonderful places tucked away in this part of the state. The shack, a relatively recent spinoff of the nearby Blount Seafood Company, is a delightful, two-trailer setup with a large circus-sized dining tent in the middle of a crushed-shell parking lot right next to the harbor in beautiful Warren, Rhode Island.

Be careful as you're driving down Water Street in Warren, since it's easy to miss the discreet street sign announcing that the Blount shack is nearby. Turn in at the sign and drive the short distance to the waterfront, where you'll find plenty of parking next to the fenced-off trailer/shacks and dining tent and the adjacent seafood and boat buildings.

**BLOUNT** Clam Shack's blockbuster menu.

Blount's cozy and casual atmosphere kicks in right away as you stroll onto the grounds. Oldies music is piped in through speakers that are strategically placed around the grounds. But don't pause to hear the music. Beat a path to the blue trailers where Blount's finest wait to take your order.

## A Shift from Oysters to Clams

Although the clam shack is only about five years old, Blount has a long and colorful history along the docks of Warren, Rhode Island. Back in the 1930s, the Narragansett Bay Oyster Company was one of several successful oyster operations on the Warren waterfront. At that time, Narragansett Bay was one of the premier oyster bed areas in the country. A powerful hurricane in 1938 that devastated much of New England ripped through the area and destroyed more than three-fourths of the region's oyster beds, permanently crippling the oyster industry in Narragansett Bay.

In 1943, Nelson Blount bought the Narragansett Bay Oyster Company's waterfront property, and he transformed the former oyster business into a clam operation. Within a few years, he bought up a few other businesses in the area and created the Blount Seafood Corporation, which today processes millions of clams annually. The clams from the Warren facility go into chowders all over the country, from big-name mass producers to gourmet restaurants and food retailers. You can see Blount's signature blue-colored processing plant and operations about a block south of the shack.

## THE MOBY-DICK OF LOBSTER ROLLS

The first thing you may notice on the menu outside the main trailer's order window is a banner announcing the Giant Lobster Roll for the princely sum of $19.95. This may seem pricey, but you get what you pay for, and with this lobster roll, you get a *lot*. Blount's giant roll contains five ounces of freshly picked, large chunks of knuckle, claw, and tail meat, served on a nine-inch toasted bun, and garnished with a flavorful dill/mayo sauce that's both slathered on the bun and drizzled on top of the lobster. The megaroll

**STEP** right up and order at Blount's main trailer shack.

comes with coleslaw and french fries. It's a complete meal and then some.

Other popular seafood rolls on the menu include the whole-belly clam roll, the clam SuperStrip roll, a scallop roll with scallops from nearby New Bedford, Massachusetts, and the albacore tuna salad roll. In all cases, you get a grilled New England–style roll, fresh-made coleslaw, and fries.

Other interesting and unusual sandwich choices include a fried haddock sandwich, a fish Reuben, and the highly unusual and tasty Fish "Taco" Wrap—a flour tortilla laden with pieces of cod, lettuce, salsa, "southwest sauce," and shredded cheese.

There is the usual assortment of deep-fried platters, but keep in mind that Blount Seafood is a premier harvester and wholesaler of clams, so a whole-belly clam or SuperStrip clam strips platter should be at or near the top of your list.

On the lighter side, you may wish to opt for Blount's Caesar salad, with fresh romaine lettuce, grated parmesan cheese, and a wonderful homemade Caesar salad dressing. Top your Caesar with Maine shrimp or lobster meat, and you've got a complete meal that hasn't been anywhere near the deep fryer.

Clam cakes are nicely done at Blount's. They're petite and lightly flecked with onion and bits of clam. They're also very light in texture and density, so ordering half a dozen is not going to cause any remorse.

## CHOWDER FROM THE EXPERTS

The chowder may be the best thing about Blount's Clam Shack. The parent company made its reputation on chowder, and the shack has benefited greatly from the seafood company's expertise in chowder making. You may order the red or white versions—both are creamy yet light with generous portions of clam and perfectly cooked chunks of potato swimming in a rich broth. If you don't feel like having a full meal, a cup or

**BLOUNT'S** friendly, youthful staff stands ready to serve you all summer long.

bowl of chowder with some clam cakes makes for a fine, light repast. Lobster bisque and lobster stew (a meal in itself) are also available.

There are two trailer/kitchens at Blount, each with a specific purpose. As you're facing them, the larger trailer to the left is the main one, where you may order anything that's on the menu. The shack's main kitchen is in here. The smaller trailer to the right is the "Express," where only clam cakes, chowder, beer, and wine are served. Both trailers are painted a deep, dark blue, the same color as the parent company's nearby building.

Once you've got food and drink in hand, head over to one of two dining areas on the shack's waterfront—the aforementioned banquet tent, which provides plenty of shade and protection from inclement weather, or any of the dozen or so open-air picnic tables situated closer to the water. No matter where you sit, you're guaranteed a gorgeous view of Warren's harbor area, which bustles with commercial and pleasure craft at all hours of the day. There's almost always a steady breeze blowing up the bay to keep things cool, and on sunny days, the rays make the choppy water sparkle in a mesmerizing sort of way.

If you're a boat owner and afloat in the area, feel free to tie up at one of the clam shack's slips and come ashore for a feast on land or some great food to go. Either way, you're in for a treat. There's live music every Sunday afternoon from 3 to 7 p.m., but if inclement weather is expected, be sure to call ahead to determine if festivities will be taking place.

One last thing to check out is the retail store a block or so away from the Warren shack, where Blount sells its signature gourmet chowders fresh and frozen, along with a new line of gourmet dips that are drawing raves from locals and tourists alike.

So, if you think trailers are trashy, think again. Blount's Clam Shack will certainly change your mind!

# Evelyn's Drive-In

2335 Main Road, Tiverton, RI 02878 | (401) 624-3100 | www.evelynsdrivein.com | Open early April to late Septem

**R**are is the eatery that gives off such comforting and radiant good vibes as Evelyn's Drive-In on Nanaquaket Pond in Tiverton, Rhode Island. There is a peaceful air to this place that is virtually unmatched among clam shacks on the New England coastline, and the food is as serene and satisfying as its surroundings. As the sign next to the kitchen order window says: IF YOU'RE IN A HURRY, YOU'RE IN THE WRONG PLACE.

## A CLAM SHACK AND MORE

Evelyn's is part clam shack, part full-service restaurant. If dining in the rough is your desire, then step up to the order window on the front side of the red-shingled building. A menu hangs overhead, and there are daily specials listed on a small chalkboard. Once you've ordered and your food is ready, you may retire to one of the ten or so picnic tables strung along the side of the pond and sheltered by a corrugated roof suspended by rustic wooden posts and boards.

It's a fine spot to sit and watch the boats and birds on the pond while you feast on Evelyn's fine and varied cuisine. There's also a dock below the sheltered tables where hungry boaters tie up and walk the wooden gangplank up to Evelyn's for a snack or a meal.

**EVELYN'S**—that cute little red shack on Nanaquaket Pond.

Your other option is to go inside, where you'll find a cozy dining room with a small counter and several tables. Exit through the building's back door and you'll be in a roped-in, crushed-shell patio area that also hugs the pond. There are a dozen or so tables with umbrellas, and wait staff is on hand to take your order and bring your food when it's ready. Just like the adjacent picnic tables, you'll have a great view of the pond and its surroundings. Particularly mesmerizing from both vantage points are the gorgeous sunsets that occur in the summertime, so you may want to time your visit to coincide with the twilight hours.

## A LITTLE BIT OF HISTORY

Evelyn Duponte opened her namesake drive-in eatery back in 1969. She ran it as a combination seafood shack and diner until she put it up for sale in the early 1990s. Current owners Domenic and Jane Bitto stumbled upon the place more or less by accident while scouting out other possible restaurant opportunities in the area. Dom's family had a background in the restaurant business, but he and Jane had been living in Boston and working more in the white-collar realm than in the kitchen. However, they fell in love with Evelyn's and decided to give it a try.

When they took over the drive-in, the Bittos kept many of Evelyn's dishes on their menu, and they began to add some of their own. Over time, this happy mix has created a menu that's both basic and unique. Evelyn still comes back from time to time for visits, and she's welcomed with open arms by the Bittos and loyal patrons with long memories.

### Evelyn's Rhode Island Clam Chowder

This is Evelyn's original recipe. It's a light and flavorful chowder—one you'll likely want to make again and again. This recipe makes 8 large servings.

INGREDIENTS

- 1 gallon cold water
- 2 cups freshly chopped raw clams
- 1 medium onion, chopped
- 1 cup unsalted butter
- 4 bay leaves
- 3 tablespoons clam base
- 1½ tablespoons salt
- ½ tablespoon ground black pepper
- 4 cups ½-inch-diced potatoes
- Half-and-half (optional)

Put all the ingredients except the potatoes and half-and-half in a large soup pot. Bring to a boil over medium-high heat. Add the potatoes and cook until tender, about 10 minutes. Ladle the soup into bowls and serve with a dollop of half-and-half, or have the chowder clear, without the half-and-half.

## ||||| SEAFOOD WITH A FLAIR |||||

First and foremost at Evelyn's is the seafood. Start off with the renowned clam cakes and one of the chowders. The clam chowder is a particularly good choice. It's the Rhode Island variety, which means it's basically a flavorful broth chock-full of clams and potatoes with a bit of milk added just before it's ladled into your bowl. The clam cakes, served by the half-dozen and dozen, are particularly light and fluffy with numerous pieces of minced clam in each one. Unlike at many other shacks, these clam cakes don't weigh you down; they only whet your appetite for more fine seafood. (If clam chowder isn't your thing, try the excellent fish chowder or the creamy lobster bisque.)

Topping the list of seafood entrees is the fried whole-belly clam plate. These golden morsels are lightly coated and delicately fried for a crispy yet chewy crunch. The accompanying french fries are thin-cut and similarly crispy, and the homemade coleslaw offers the perfect cool complement to the piping hot seafood and fries. Similar seafood plates feature sea scallops, crab cakes (with zesty horseradish sauce), clam strips, cod, or shrimp. You may also get a combo plate, which features a mix of scallops and clams. Then there's the hefty, two-pound seafood platter, more than enough deep-fried splendor for two hungry diners.

There are also a number of baked and grilled seafood dinners, including a very tasty fillet of sole stuffed with crab and scallops, a grilled salmon fillet, grilled shrimp, and a particularly fine plate of pan-grilled sea scallops, again served with Evelyn's trademark horseradish sauce.

Perhaps the most exotic item on the menu (and one of the most talked about and most popular) is the Lobster Chow Mein. This dish is an Evelyn Duponte original, and the Bittos have kept it on the menu to

**EVELYN'S** peaceful back patio, as viewed from the shack's boat dock.

the joy of many longstanding customers. They basically take some crispy noodles, ladle chow mein gravy (that's what they call it) over the noodles, and then top it off with several chunks of fresh lobster meat. It may sound strange (especially because we're in eastern Rhode Island, not Manhattan), but it's a flavor and texture combination that works to great effect.

Seafood rolls are popular here, with the lobster roll topping the list. You may have yours with either cold mayo or melted butter, both of which are served on the side so that you may customize your roll in whatever manner you wish. In addition to the clam, scallop, clam strip, and crab rolls, Evelyn's also has a couple of interesting seafood wraps as well as several tasty, healthy entrée-size salads.

## Other Must-Haves

More on the diner side of things are such choices as the hearty meat loaf platter, the chicken pie, and the breaded fried chicken breast, all served with an amazingly substantial and flavorful side of homemade mashed potatoes and fresh, locally grown vegetables.

In addition to the fine pies and sundaes on the dessert menu, the standout item has to be Evelyn's famed Grape Nut Pudding. This New England taste treat is a custard-type concoction with good, old-fashioned Grape Nuts cereal, dashes of cinnamon and nutmeg, and a dollop of whipped cream on top. (The recipe for Evelyn's version is featured in Brooke Dojny's *New England Clam Shack Cookbook,* in case you want to try making it at home.)

Once you've had your fill at Evelyn's, kick back, relax, and enjoy the cooling breezes and the sparkling water as you gaze contentedly on Nanaquaket Pond—and, if you time it right, wait for the sunset.

### "Is This Heaven?"

At one point in the movie *Field of Dreams*, the ghost of Shoeless Joe Jackson turns to Kevin Costner in Costner's cornfield-cum-ball-park and asks him, "Is this heaven?" Costner smiles and replies, "No, it's Iowa."

Similarly, when you find yourself seated at one of Dom and Jane Bitto's waterfront tables, taking in the serenity of Nanaquaket Pond after a fine meal, you may feel moved to ask them the same question, to which they would contentedly reply, "No, it's Evelyn's."

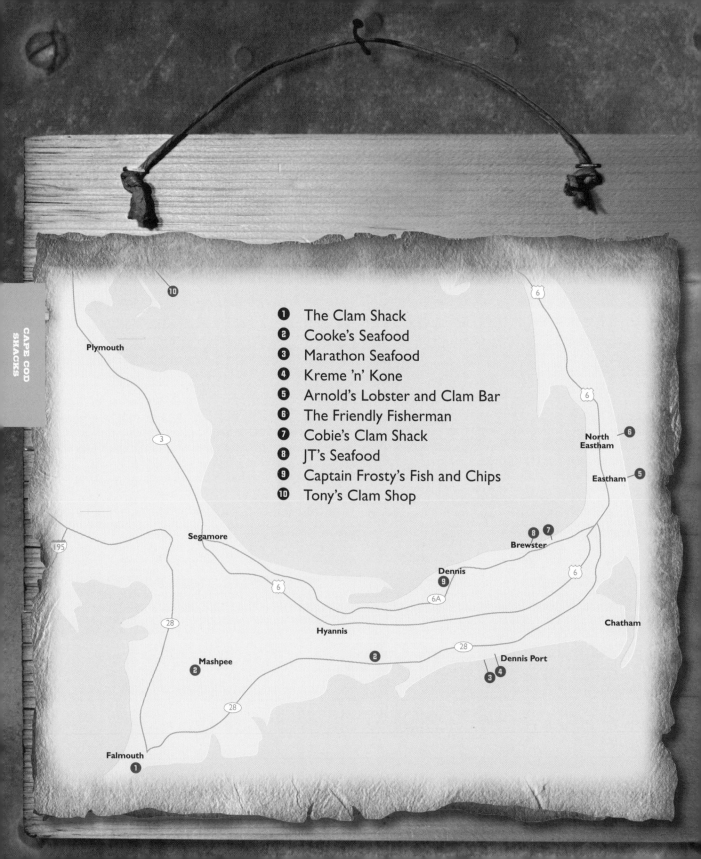

1 The Clam Shack
2 Cooke's Seafood
3 Marathon Seafood
4 Kreme 'n' Kone
5 Arnold's Lobster and Clam Bar
6 The Friendly Fisherman
7 Cobie's Clam Shack
8 JT's Seafood
9 Captain Frosty's Fish and Chips
10 Tony's Clam Shop

Plymouth

Segamore

North Eastham

Eastham

Brewster

Dennis

Hyannis

Chatham

Mashpee

Dennis Port

Falmouth

# CAPE COD SHACKS

**C**ape Cod and clam shacks go together like peanut butter and jelly (actually, more like clam cakes and chowder). And there is no better way to tackle your craving for seafood on the Cape than by stopping into any one of the many quality shacks that line the highways and dot the harbors in this summertime vacationland.

There's a wide variety of clam shacks to choose from, depending on your tastes and your budget. Some are modest, weathered roadside takeout-type places with a few picnic tables scattered about the grounds, while others are full-blown fried seafood palaces with gleaming order counters; dozens of young workers manning the counter, kitchen, and grounds; and seating indoors and out for hundreds at a time.

One thing you can be guaranteed: the seafood you get on the Cape will be as fresh and well prepared as it can be. There are two reasons for this: First, much of the seafood served at Cape Cod clam shacks is harvested nearby, so it travels from boat to plate in no time flat. Second, if you're not serving good, fresh, thoughtfully prepared seafood on Cape Cod, you're not going to be in business for long. The competition is just too darned intense.

So, it's a buyer's market on the Cape, even in peak season, as shack owners vie for your business with specials and coupons and entertainment that they hope will keep you coming back for more.

# The Clam Shack

227 Clinton Avenue, Falmouth, MA 02540 | (508) 540-7758 | Open late May to early September

This small, unassuming shack on the dock in Falmouth harbor at the base of Cape Cod looks diminutive from the street, but if you happen to go around back and get a look at it from the water, it's notably larger, both in size and reputation. This is because many of the Clam Shack's steadiest and most loyal customers come from the boats that ply the waters of Vineyard Sound and Falmouth Harbor as well as the numerous tourists who embark for Martha's Vineyard from the schooners that dock right next to the shack. If this were a bus terminal in the 1950s, then the Clam Shack would be the cute little diner next door with great comfort food for all the weary travelers.

**THE** Clam Shack's bare-bones menu is deceptively simple.

## A No-Nonsense Menu

The Clam Shack has one of the most basic menus of any shack on the New England coast.

This allows father-and-son owners James and Matthew Limberakis to do only a few things—and they do them very well. Whereas many shacks have added baked and grilled seafood items and ice cream and smoothies to their menus, the Clam Shack prefers to stick close to the deep fryer for seafood and snacks and to the grill for burgers, hot dogs, and grilled cheese.

The Clam Shack's fried clams consistently win top honors in many of the Cape's best-fried-clams competitions, which are conducted annually by local food editors at various publications or extracted from reader surveys and polls. The plump, crispy whole bellies are fried up in fresh-daily oil, as is all the other fried seafood (strips, scallops, shrimp, and fish and chips only). All the deep-fried seafood is served up by the box or as part of a plate that includes french fries and coleslaw.

As for seafood sandwiches, the cold lobster

**THE** Clam Shack's rough-hewn exterior blends in perfectly with its harbor setting.

roll is another winner, heaped high with fresh lobster meat on a toasted split-top bun. This is one of the best-selling items at the Clam Shack. There's also a clam roll, a scallop roll, and a fish sandwich.

From the grill, you may choose between hamburgers, cheeseburgers, grilled hot dogs, and grilled cheese. These also come in the form of plates with fries and slaw. As for snacks, there are onion rings, clam chowder, cheese sticks, and chicken tenders.

And that's about it. The choices are few, but everything is delicious.

## DOCKSIDE DINING

One of the joys of coming down to the Clam Shack is the opportunity to sit at a picnic table out on the dock and enjoy your meal while watching all the fishing boats and pleasure craft come and go. There's a small dining area inside the shack, but seating is limited, and it's much nicer outside on a sunny day.

Perhaps the best place to enjoy your repast is on the second-floor deck on the back of the Clam Shack, where there are several picnic tables overlooking the harbor. The sight lines up here are great, as you can see well out into Vineyard Sound. There's an outdoor staircase on the side of the building that gives you access, but the deck can often be crowded during lunch and dinner hours, so plan on arriving early.

The Limberakis family has been serving up great food at this hard-to-find spot for over fifty years. Here's hoping they keep it up for at least fifty more!

# Cooke's Seafood

1120 Iyannough Road, Hyannis, MA 02601 | (508) 775-0450 | 7 Ryan's Way, Mashpee, MA 02649 | (508) 477-9595 | www.cookesseafood.com | Open February through November

There are certain clam shacks on Cape Cod that have been so successful over the years that they've grown to become major multi-destination restaurants for thousands of summer tourists. That's not to say that such places should necessarily be bypassed for smaller, quainter shacks. Au contraire, some of these big boys serve the best, most consistently fresh seafood to be found on the Cape. What you may sometimes lose in charm you more than make up for in gastronomic satisfaction.

## TWO LOCATIONS, ONE FINE MENU

Cooke's Seafood is just such an establishment. With two locations, one in Hyannis, the other in Mashpee, Cooke's is a major player in the upper and mid-Cape. Both locations feature spacious, clean dining rooms that look almost like banquet halls with booths lining the walls, sconce-like chandeliers hanging from the ceilings, and picture windows wrapping around three sides of the dining room. It's a somewhat impersonal dining experience in comparison to smaller mom-and-pop operations found on the Cape. But the sheer volume of cooking that Cooke's does each day allows them to offer wonderfully fresh seafood at very reasonable prices.

There are several deep fryers in each kitchen, and they're going full bore throughout the summer, frying up clams, clam strips, scallops, calamari, onion rings, and much more. In addition, there's an extensive offering

**COOKE'S** cavernous dining room at its Mashpee location.

of healthier broiled, baked, and grilled seafood platters as well as steamed 1 1/4-pound lobsters in season. Seafood rolls, burgers, and various fish and chicken sandwiches round out the offerings.

## Awards and Conquests

Despite its rather pedestrian look and feel, Cooke's consistently wins awards from various newspapers and reader's polls every year for the freshness and quality of its seafood. For instance, Cooke's was awarded the Best Fried Clams on the Cape five years in a row by local radio station WCOD. In addition, they've been voted Best in Seafood by poll takers in the *Cape Cod Life* survey nearly every year since 1993.

Further proof of Cooke's dominance in the local seafood scene occurred when a Red Lobster opened across the street from Cooke's Hyannis location. After only fifteen months, Red Lobster shut down and left town, unable to compete with Cooke's superior quality and customer service. So, although Cooke's may give the appearance of a somewhat impersonal chain-type operation, be assured that this family-owned and -operated two-outlet shack can deliver some of the best seafood you'll find anywhere up and down the Cape.

## Seafood Sam's: Another Fine Chain of Shacks

There's another constellation of high-volume, top-quality clam shacks under the name of Seafood Sam's that, like Cooke's Seafood, are strung out across the Cape and serve up loads of great seafood. The three Seafood Sam's locations guarantee that you're never far from one in the mid- and upper Cape areas. They're located in the towns of Sandwich (just over the Sagamore bridge spanning the Cape Cod Canal), Falmouth (not far from Cooke's Mashpee location), and on busy Route 28 in South Yarmouth at the nexus of the mid-Cape's bustling beach and shopping scenes.

Seafood Sam's got its start in 1974 in an old laundromat that was gutted and fitted out with a couple of deep fryers by Sam Vecchione and his nephew Paul Colonero. With a secret recipe for seasoning the seafood and a lot of hard work, Seafood Sam's has become a Cape Cod tradition with hundreds of traveling families each year who come back repeatedly for great seafood at bargain prices.

# Marathon Seafood

231 Main Street, West Dennis, MA 02673 | (508) 394-3379 | www.marathonseafoodcapecod.com
**Open year-round**

**S**ituated on the south side of Route 28, the main east-west highway that cuts through the southern portion of Cape Cod, Marathon Seafood has been serving up deep-fried clams and more to Cape Cod locals and tourists year-round for nearly three decades. Next to the Bass River in the town of West Dennis, Marathon is perfectly positioned to pull in seafood-hungry motorists with its huge sign out front and its ample parking lot along the east side of the building.

As the name seems to suggest, this clam shack is owned and operated by a dedicated, hard-working Greek-American family. Ted and Peggy Stoilas opened Marathon in 1983, and they've presided over it ever since. Hard work and long hours have helped them build a steady clientele, and their Greek touches on a number of dishes help to set them apart from many of the other seafood emporiums along crowded and competitive Route 28.

## The Quality of Quantity

This is a no-nonsense place with the look and feel of a 1970s coffee shop. The dining room consists of a number of open-ended, molded plastic and metal hardback booths riveted to the floor. The wings of the dining area have a handful of regular wooden tables, each seating anywhere from two to six diners. A lengthy vine snakes its way above the windows, and it pretty much wraps its way around the entire room.

In somewhat stark contrast to the otherwise subdued setting is the large black-and-white-and-red illuminated menu that dominates the wall behind the order counter in the main room. It lists in almost overwhelming fashion the numerous lunch and dinner options available, so you should take your time and study it carefully.

Quantity is king here. The gigantic seafood platters, which come with fries, onion rings, and coleslaw, dominate the menu and are very popular with the regulars. The seafood combination platter is stacked so high, you'll be thankful it comes on a large paper plate that is supported by a plastic cafeteria tray to catch the fries, rings, and shellfish that come tumbling down the deep-fried mountainside as you dig in. Alternatives to this belt-busting meal for two (or more) diners include a two-fish combo platter (pick any two you like) or the more modest single-item platters of whole-belly or strip clams, scallops, fried fish, oysters, calamari, or shrimp. Be forewarned, however, that all the platters are gargantuan, so ordering sides of chowder or poppers or mozzarella sticks is almost certainly going to be superfluous.

## TRY THE GREEK GOODIES

One side dish, however, in which you should indulge is Teddy's locally famous Greek salad. Go with the large if you want to make a meal of it, and opt for the small as a refreshing addition to your deep-fried main course. Fresh shredded lettuce, cucumber, tomato, onion, and feta cheese are great antidotes to an otherwise high-calorie repast. Ted also makes his own baklava, a nutty, flaky, honey-coated Greek confection that's not to be missed.

In recent years, other light alternatives have been added to the menu. Broiled seafood dinners are particularly popular and are served with sides of fresh vegetables and rice or various forms of potatoes or onion rings. Greek-style lamb chops, pork chops, broiled chicken, and souvlaki (kebabs) round out the alternative offerings that steer clear of Marathon's deep fryers.

Bottom line: If you and your family are cruising on Route 28 in Dennis and you need to fill up quickly and cheaply on your way to or from the beach, Marathon's a good bet to satisfy everyone in your hungry crew.

**FEAST** your eyes (then your belly) on the multitudinous menu offerings at Marathon Seafood.

# Kream 'n' Kone

961 Route 28, West Dennis, MA 02639 | (508) 394-0808 | www.kreamnkone.com
Open mid-February to late October

This may be the hardest-working shack on the Cape. Owners Angela and Angelo Argyriadis have put their blood, sweat, and tears into this bustling seafood stand, growing it from its humble shack roots into an expansive, clean, and friendly eatery strategically located at the nexus of Routes 28 and 134 in the heart of one of Cape Cod's busiest tourist areas.

Angela and Angelo take their business very seriously, and they watch over it with vigilance and tender loving care from the time they open

KREAM 'n' Kone's order counter stretches some fifty feet across the shack's front room.

in mid-February (earlier than most seasonal shacks) until they close in late October. All their hard work and constant fussing over the fine details means you can count on the Kream 'n' Kone to deliver some of the best fried seafood on the Cape.

## HUMBLE BEGINNINGS

Way back in 1953, a couple of guys opened an ice-cream and burger stand on Route 28 in Dennisport and named it the Kream 'n' Kone. The unusual name with its misspellings was intentional in order to be different (think Jell-O or Toys R Us). Initially ice cream, burgers, and hot dogs were the only things they served. After several years, they noticed that other stands on busy Route 28 were installing deep fryers, expanding into fried seafood, and pulling in lots of curious, hungry customers. They decided to do the same with the K 'n' K, and the shack's future course was set. Despite the major change in business strategy and focus, the funny ice-cream stand name stuck, and it's remained the Kream 'n' Kone for nearly sixty years.

## Rising from the Ashes

As tourism grew on the Cape, so did the Kream 'n' Kone, as it went through a succession of owners until 1989, when the Argyriadises bought the business and ran it for the next few years. Then, on March 6, 1993, a fire tore through the Kream 'n' Kone, destroying 70 percent of the building and rendering it uninhabitable.

Rather than pack it in for the year and mull over their options, Angelo and Angela quickly scouted around for a new location and found an Italian restaurant for sale less than a mile to the west on Route 28, and they bought it. With the help of family and friends, they quickly converted the building into the new home of Kream 'n' Kone, and they were back in business just in time for the July Fourth holiday that same year.

Over time, the Argyriadises have added on to the building, creating a spacious, clean, airy, two-level, three-sectioned dining room. With cane-back chairs, knotty pine window trim, and potted silk plants, the Kream 'n' Kone of today is almost elegant.

## It's All in the Ingredients

Angelo is fanatical about the seafood he purchases from suppliers, checking each shipment that comes in every day. He attributes much of Kream 'n' Kone's success and popularity to persnickety seafood procurement. Kream 'n' Kone's award-winning clams come from Ipswich, and each shipment is hand-inspected by Angelo himself before being accepted. The large, meaty sea scallops come from scallop boats out of New Bedford, and the lobster meat used in the lobster rolls (no whole lobsters served here) comes from the famed Lobster Trap of Maine.

Fried whole-belly clams are clearly a standout here. They've won numerous awards from *Cape Cod Life* (check out the displays on the wall by the front door) and with good reason. They're plump, lightly breaded, crispy, and golden brown, and they match up very nicely with fries and onion rings on the seafood plate.

Other excellent choices at Kream 'n' Kone include the scallop plate, the meaty lobster roll, and the broiled flounder dinner, served with rice pilaf, coleslaw, and a wedge of lemon. There are plenty of non-seafood sandwiches, such as burgers, grilled chicken, and hot dogs, and several meal-size salads to choose from, including a particularly nice Greek salad loaded with feta cheese and kalamata olives.

With its enviable location at the corner of Routes 28 and 134, Kream 'n' Kone is perfectly situated to serve anyone vacationing in the mid-Cape region. Through hard work and perseverance, they can truly make a strong claim to the fifty-year-old slogan on their sign out front: "The Finest Fried Seafood Anywhere."

# Arnold's Lobster & Clam Bar

3580 Route 6, Eastham, MA 02642 | (508) 255-2575 | www.arnoldsrestaurant.com
Open mid-May to mid-October

Chances are you'll see the line of customers snaking out of Arnold's front door and lingering beneath the yellow-and-white awning before you see much of the restaurant itself. This combination clam shack, lobster pound, raw bar, and ice-cream stand is justifiably one of the most popular eateries on the entire Cape, and the crowds on a warm summer day can be enormous.

What makes this place so popular? For one thing, the encyclopedic menu of seafood items to choose from. You name it, Arnold's has it—salads, chowders, bisques, lobsters, baked dinners, a raw bar, fried baskets, seafood rolls (fried and otherwise), and a variety of non-seafood sandwich offerings. In addition, there's a full-service bar serving beer, wine, and mixed drinks and an eighteen-hole championship miniature golf course adjacent to the shack.

You want more? Check out the ice-cream stand on the side of the building, which serves up hard and soft ice cream, sundaes, splits, brownies, and chocolate chip cookies. You can eat, you can drink, you can putt, or you can simply sit back and take it all in, as there's never a dull moment or quiet time at this bustling mega-shack.

**ARNOLD'S** keeps hopping well into the summer nights.

## How It All Got Started

Way back in the early 1950s, there was a small hot dog stand named Whitey's where Arnold's currently sits. Whitey's morphed into Gertrude's Beach Box (famous for Gertrude's clam cakes) in 1956, and it carried on, serving seafood and sandwiches, for another twenty years when it was purchased by Cape Cod native Nate Nickerson III in 1977. Nickerson came up with the name Arnold's, which he borrowed from Arnold's Drive-In of TV's *Happy Days* fame. Arnold's began as a rather unusual drive-in clam shack, complete with deep-fried seafood, roller-skating carhop waitresses, and an overall 1950s look and feel to the place.

A fire destroyed the drive-in shack in 1993, and it gave Nickerson a chance to rethink and rebuild Arnold's from scratch. With an eye to the future, he increased the size of the building, added an ice-cream stand onto the side, and gave the place a more contemporary, family-type look and feel. Today, Arnold's is a sprawling complex of rooms, patios, tents, and order windows capable of accommodating hundreds of hungry customers at a time.

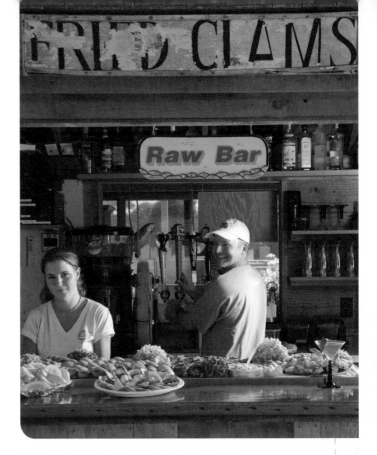

**THE** raw bar at Arnold's—a shack within a shack.

## ABOUT THOSE LINES ...

Long lines are the norm at Arnold's, and they can be daunting when you see them winding back into the parking lot. Take comfort in knowing that the kitchen and the service counters inside are hyper-efficient and will keep the lines moving at an incredibly rapid rate, minimizing your wait time and any resultant despair. The best thing to do while waiting in line is to grab a lavish color menu and begin narrowing down what you want to order from all the wonderful things that Arnold's has to offer.

To begin, the New England clam chowder is excellent—thick, creamy, and full of clams and potatoes—but a cup is enough so that you may save room for your main course. If you're not in the mood for chowder, consider splitting an order of Arnold's famous onion rings with your dining mates as an appetizer. These thin-cut, battered beauties are crispy, crunchy, sweet—everything onion rings should be. Some people come here just for the rings, and they leave very happy. One other opening option is to try a salad. Most are meal-size, so consider sharing or having one as your entrée. The Nantucket

## Sesame Encrusted Salmon with Orange Miso Sauce

This is one of Arnold's baked salmon daily specials, which appears regularly on the menu. It may seem a little highbrow for clam shack fare, but it's so simple to make and so tasty that you'll be glad you gave it a try.

INGREDIENTS

- 1 cup mayonnaise
- 1 tablespoon sesame oil, plus more for cooking salmon
- 1 teaspoon finely chopped ginger
- 1 heaping tablespoon white miso
- 3 tablespoons frozen orange juice
- 1 teaspoon orange zest
- 3 pounds of salmon fillets
- Sesame seeds
- Orange slices (optional)

For orange miso sauce, in a medium bowl, add all the ingredients except the salmon and sesame seeds and hand-whip. Set aside.
For salmon fillets, brush on a little sesame oil and sprinkle with sesame seeds. Cook in a 450-degree F oven for 10 minutes. Drizzle the orange miso sauce over the salmon when serving and top with a thin slice of orange for garnish, if desired.

Strawberry Spinach Salad is the standout, with strawberries, blueberries, almonds, sesame seeds, mandarin orange slices, and a balsamic apple cider vinaigrette.

Lobsters here are served in a variety of sizes up to, and even over, three pounds. These fresh-caught crustaceans are locally harvested and brought in daily, steamed, and served with your choice of corn on the cob, clam chowder, and/or a pound of steamers (and drawn butter, of course). Interestingly, Arnold's Maryland-style crab cakes are one of the most popular items after lobster, and they're served with an innovative avocado salsa.

On the deep-fried side, the whole bellies reign supreme, piled high on a dinner platter with french fries and coleslaw. Rounding out Arnold's all-star team of main courses is the lobster roll, served cold with a bit of mayo and piled high on a toasted split-top bun. The fresh-picked meat cascades down the sides of the roll, ready for you to pick up with your fingers and pop into your mouth.

## BANQUET HALLS AND BUZZERS

Once you've placed your order at the bustling counter, you'll be given an electronic buzzer, which gives you the freedom to roam the grounds in search of the perfect table, knowing that you don't have to hover around and wait for your number to be called. When your little black box begins to buzz, head back and pick up your food.

The dining areas at Arnold's (there are four of them) are varied and inviting. Just off the service counter area is an indoor dining room with some twenty Formica-topped tables and wooden chairs. Side-sliding windows allow for breezes to circulate through and keep you cool. A shingled shed-type service bar with cocktails, beer, wine, and raw clams and oysters juts into the room like a shack within a shack, catering to those who want raw seafood or spirits.

If you wish to be closer to the outdoors, simply walk out the back of the dining room into a yellow-and-white canopied patio that has twenty or so tables, many equipped with seating to accommodate up to six diners. The patio spills into a tented area with open sides and about a dozen picnic tables for larger parties. Finally, for a more intimate experience, there's a tree-shaded spot in the far back of Arnold's with about ten or so tables and umbrellas for couples and other small parties.

## How About Some Ice Cream?

The fire in the early 1990s had the unintended consequence of allowing Nate to rethink and expand upon the original drive-in. A large, canopied ice-cream stand became part of the new setup, with order and pickup windows and lots of outdoor seating nearby. You may choose from the usual lineup of cones, sundaes, shakes, and other frozen delights. It's a great (if sinful) way to top off a fine deep-fried seafood meal. The bike racks next to the ice-cream window are often filled with cycles owned by pedalers who have decamped from the nearby Cape Cod Bike Trail, which runs in back of Arnold's, and stopped in for a cone at the shady oasis.

Lobster, clams, grilled sandwiches, onion rings, mini golf, ice cream, bike trails—what's not to like at Arnold's? This is a destination clam shack if ever there was one.

### Golf, Anyone?

Miniature golf, that is. Arnold's owner Nate Nickerson has constructed an extravagant eighteen-hole course adjacent to the shack, and it's as scenic as it is challenging. With waterfalls and bridges and lots of other playful obstacles, kids love to swarm over the lighted course night and day. You can get a gallery-type view of several of the holes from Arnold's adjacent string of outdoor patios and dining areas.

# The Friendly Fisherman

4580 State Highway, North Eastham, MA 02651 | (508) 255-3009 | www.friendlyfishermaneastham.com
Open early May through mid-October

As traffic begins to taper off on northbound Route 6 in the Lower Cape and you embark on the scenic drive towards Provincetown, keep an eye out on the right-hand side of the road in North Eastham for the cedar-shingled Friendly Fisherman. This is another seafood combo operation—equal parts fish/produce market and clam shack. Cofounder and owner Janet Demetri is the queen of the castle at this fun and funky roadside establishment, which has been selling seafood in one form or another from the same spot for over twenty years.

Janet and her husband Michael first opened the Friendly Fisherman in the spring of 1989, at around the same time that their daughter Alana was born. Michael passed away in 2006, and Alana has stepped up and joined forces with her mother to keep this one-of-a-kind eatery and market prospering.

When Friendly Fisherman first opened, it was just a seafood market doing a brisk business with locals and tourists alike, always drawing raves for its unusually fresh fish. Janet and Michael had scouted out the best, most reliable fishermen and lobstermen in the area, and they received the best of the catches on the Lower Cape every day.

Shortly after opening, the Demetris thought it would be fun (and profitable) to add a deep-fried seafood operation to their roadside stand, so an addition was tacked on to the building, giving the new, enlarged structure an L shape with a gravel parking lot in front and picnic tables along the side. A roofed, open-air dining section and awning were later added to the side of the shack by the order windows, and additional picnic tables were sprinkled around the side and back to complete the scene as it looks today.

**FRIENDLY** Fisherman owner Janet Demetri.

**STOP** by the Friendly Fisherman for some great fresh seafood and fried clams.

## COLORFUL, NAUTICAL OUTDOOR DINING

One of the nicest things about Friendly Fisherman is the inviting picnic area with its colorfully table-clothed outdoor tables and the copious lobster buoys and fishing nets hanging all over the surrounding fences. There's also a small but adorable childrens' play area in back, with a huge truck tire and a painted sign showing three lobsters, with holes in the sign where kiddies can stick their faces through for unforgettable family photos. The atmosphere is trés casual, and you will see fellow diners in all sorts of attire, including lots of bathing suits, as the Cape Cod National Seashore is nearby. Friendly Fisherman is a BYO establishment, and there's a liquor store conveniently located next door, should you feel in the mood.

## FRESH AND TASTY SEAFOOD, ALWAYS AND FOREVER

The Demetris have taken more than twenty years to perfect their recipes, and it shows in the high quality of their deep-fried fare. The whole-belly clams are unusually light and sweet with juicy bellies that melt in your mouth. Scallops are of local origin and are uniformly crisp, nicely breaded, and firm. The fillets in their fish and chips are taken from the seafood market, where some of the best fresh fish on the Cape is delivered on a daily basis. Janet and her staff buy their fish whole and fillet them throughout the day, guaranteeing freshness both in the market and at the shack.

Like at many seafood stands, the lobster roll rules supreme in terms of popularity and overall sales here. Rachael Ray stopped by on her way back to the mainland from Provincetown a couple of years ago, and she gave the roll a rave in her magazine, carrying on about the copious amounts of sweet lobster meat mixed with a light amount of mayo and piled so high she could barely find the bun. (Ray, by the way, was born on the Cape and is somewhat of an expert when it comes to New England seafood, so this is high praise indeed.)

There's a fisherman's platter at the Friendly Fisherman that seems a little scary at $34.95, ten dollars more than at other places on the Cape. But there's plenty of deep-fried seafood for two, maybe even three, hungry people, so the more companions you get to help you finish it off, the more of a bargain it'll turn out to be.

## A Peek at the Market

Chances are you're only planning on grabbing a bite to eat when you stop by the Friendly Fisherman. But even if you're not in the market or the mood for fresh fish, you should check out the quaint, cozy, and beautifully stocked and decorated little store next to the shack. Inside you'll find beautifully cut fish fillets from the morning's catch, along with lots of shellfish, fresh lobsters, pastas, locally harvested produce, and fresh baked goods. This definitely beats anything you'll find at any supermarket on the Cape, and you should really consider picking something up before taking off. Between the market and the clam shack, the Demetris have a class act going here. It's truly a diamond in the rough just off the road to Provincetown and well worth a visit.

### Customers Say the Darnedest Things

Janet Demetri has been behind the counter as owner of the Friendly Fisherman for more than twenty years. Here's a short list of things that she swears her customers have asked or said to her over the years:

- ✪ "Instead of chips with the fish and chips, can I get french fries?"
- ✪ "The Maryland blue crabs—where do they come from?"
- ✪ "I want my money back. I ordered the whole-belly clams, and you gave me fried steamers."
- ✪ "What kind of fish is in the tuna roll?"
- ✪ "What kind of fish is in the crab cakes?"
- ✪ "Do you have turkey gravy?"

# Cobie's Clam Shack

**3260 Main Street, Brewster, MA 02631 | (508) 896-7021 | www.cobies.com**
**Open May through mid-September**

obie's is one of those pleasant surprises that you encounter when traveling on Route 6A through the picturesque town of Brewster on Cape Cod Bay. It appears as you round a bend in the road—a plain-looking, neatly kept, gray-shingled building with white trim and black shutters and a small wooden sign bearing the shack's name on a post out front. Owner Rob Slavin explains that the strict zoning laws in Brewster call for nearly every building along the town's main street to be tastefully neutral in color and trim, in keeping with the town's understated, dignified nature. Cobie's certainly lives up to the local requirements.

Though it looks diminutive from the road (Brewster frowns on large buildings as well as ostentatious facades along 6A), Cobie's is actually a rather spacious shack, much of it stretching around and behind the front with a multi-tiered deck and tables and umbrellas for relaxing and noshing. Plus, there's a very busy order window for ice cream just to the right of the food ordering area and an adjacent string of covered, open-air picnic tables stretching along the front

**LINING** up for the good stuff at Cobie's.

parking area that faces Main Street/6A. Few shacks in New England are as clean or as well run as this place, and it's a testament to Slavin's tireless efforts to provide a pleasant and memorable clam shack dining experience.

## (NOT NECESSARILY) CHANGING WITH THE TIMES

Cobie's came into being in 1948 when Coburn Emery, aka Cobie, first opened for business in a building very similar to the current one. Cape Cod was a much simpler place back then, and much has changed since—but not so much at

Cobie's. The same basic formula for success is in place: keep things commendably simple in the clam shack tradition, be as family-friendly as you can be, and emphasize friendly service, cleanliness, and consistently high-quality food.

The shack went through several rounds of ownership changes before it was purchased by Slavin and his father in 1986. Initially a schoolteacher in West Haven, Connecticut, Rob started spending his summers working with his dad at Cobie's before deciding to move permanently to Brewster in 1996 in order to make the shack his full-time endeavor. Slavin has stayed involved with teaching as a local youth volleyball coach during the fall and winter months. But come early March, it's time to start sprucing up Cobie's exterior in anticipation of opening day in May, so there's very little down-time for this busy shack or its owner.

In one nod to modern times, Cobie's has electronic beepers that they hand out to let you know when your order is ready. This allows you to stake out a spot on the decks in back or at the picnic tables

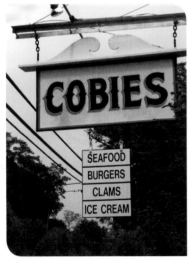

**COBIE'S** simple, understated road sign.

on the side and wait for your food in a leisurely manner, without having to hover around the pickup window.

## TASTY DISHES, OLD AND NEW

Golden, deep-fried, breaded clams are one of several specialties for which Cobie's is known. Other popular deep-fried seafood items include the fish and chips and the fried scallops. The onion rings are battered and flash-fried to make them light and crispy; they make a nice complement to virtually any dish coming out of Cobie's kitchen. The oil used in the deep fryers is 100 percent trans-fat free, and Rob changes it daily to ensure freshness and pure flavor in all the deep-fried food.

If deep-fried fare isn't for you, the lobster roll is your next best choice. It consists of all freshly picked knuckle meat that's been lightly tossed in mayo and is served cold on a toasted New England hot dog bun. Speaking of hot dogs, the foot-long wieners are big sellers here, along with Cobie's signature half-pound charbroiled black Angus burgers. New England–style clam chowder is another alternative to deep-fried seafood. Try it in a Cobie's bread bowl, a full meal in itself.

Slavin has bolstered the healthier side of his menu with the recent additions of grilled panini sandwiches, broiled scallops, and homemade clam pie. There are whole wheat wraps stuffed with snow crab or all-white chicken meat; grilled tuna, salmon, swordfish, and mahi mahi; and panko haddock—a fillet of haddock broiled and garnished with light and crispy panko bread crumbs and a touch of oregano. These new dishes are equally easy on the wallet and the waistline.

## ICE CREAM AND SMOOTHIES

Cobie's does a good bit of business from its ice-cream window, and with good reason. For starters, you can choose between regular and soft serve ice cream in a variety of flavors. The "hard" ice cream comes in about a dozen different flavors, and there are weekly special flavors throughout the season. The soft serve comes in the standard vanilla, chocolate, and swirl, as well as more than twenty other flavors, including strawberry, cranberry (a local favorite), and butterscotch. If you can't find a flavor that suits your mood, chances are it's not an ice-cream kind of day for you.

## ONE IF BY LAND, TWO IF BY BIKE TRAIL

Most people come to Cobie's via automobile on Route 6A, but an increasing number are arriving from the Cape Cod Bike Trail, which runs just south of the shack. The trail is strategically connected to Cobie's via a spur route leading from the trail to Cobie's order window. Ever on the lookout for new customers, Rob has installed a permanent sign on his property next to the trail, inviting cyclists to pedal over for a meal or a cone or just a cool beverage and a shady place to sit and rest.

Whether by car or by bike or even on foot, it's hard to resist the siren song of Cobie's on a warm summer day.

# JT's Seafood

2689 Main Street, Brewster, MA 02631 | (508) 896-3355 | www.jt-seafood.com
Open late April to late September

**H**eading through Brewster on scenic Route 6A, there's a stately, sage-colored, one-and-a-half-story clapboard building on the north side of the road that looks like an upscale restaurant. With its dark green and gold awnings, bright-gold-lettered signs, and overall hyper-neat appearance, you might expect the place to have leather banquettes inside and valet parking out front. Don't be fooled. This is JT's Seafood, an admittedly upscale clam shack and ice-cream stand where deep-fried and grilled seafood, sundaes and cones, beer and wine, and dining in the rough are as fancy as it gets.

Husband-and-wife team Bud and Cary Noyes became owners of JT's in 2004, and the business has been steadily growing and prospering ever since. The building was originally two structures separated by a breezeway; one half was a clam shack and the other was a seafood market. Ownership changed hands in 1998, and it became an Italian restaurant that was converted into a single building. When Bud and Cary took over, they went back to the clam shack motif, added ice cream to the mix, and gave the place a major facelift, in keeping with the upscale tone of the surrounding neighborhood.

A self-professed "A-type personality and neat freak," Bud arrives each morning at 5 a.m. to get things up and running, and he is constantly on the move throughout the day. Along with Cary and their children, JT's staff consists of a couple of Caribbean cooks and a rotating group of high-energy college students who are constantly hustling to accommodate the summertime crowds.

**JT'S** is one of the most elegant looking shacks in all of New England.

## The Lay of the Land

JT's is meticulously designed to offer a variety of casual dining environments, all within a relatively compact amount of space. Out front, there are several tables with classy cloth umbrellas in case you wish to enjoy the street scene passing by on 6A while you dine. Once you've entered through JT's front door, you find yourself at the order counter, which runs for some twenty feet along the right-hand side of the entryway. Across from the counter is an enclosed dining room with booths and tables on two levels and tastefully decorated with nautical artwork on the walls. If you walk straight back past the counter or through the dining room, you'll find yourself on the shady and spacious rear deck, which has several picnic tables elevated above the rear parking lot. Stake out your preferred spot from any of these three locations, then head back to the order counter and let the feast begin.

## Ready, Set, Order!

While you're waiting to place your order, check out the maps on the walls in the order area. They're festooned with pushpins showing from where JT's customers have hailed over the years. The New England map is thick with colorful pins, and the U.S. and world maps are impressively dotted as well. If these maps are true representations of JT's customers' origins, then the shack has drawn a truly a national and international crowd through its doors to enjoy their fine seafood. (There are a couple of pins stuck in Antarctica and Greenland, which makes one wonder . . .)

In keeping with the true dining-in-the-rough experience, there's a helpful menu posted above the counter. Deep-fried items still reign supreme here, especially the locally harvested whole-belly clams, the oysters and scallops from nearby Wellfleet, and the native cod from Chatham, a town located on the "elbow" of Cape Cod. The breading is light and mildly seasoned (hats off to the Caribbean chefs), and the same deep-fried magic is performed on JT's locally famous onion rings—thin-cut, lightly breaded, and served in heaping quantities. (A large order makes a great appetizer for three or four people.)

Bud and Cary have been adding some healthier alternatives in recent years, such as wraps, salads, and baked and grilled seafood dishes. Of particular note are the healthy and tasty whole wheat wraps, which come stuffed with your choice of turkey, chicken salad, crabmeat, or tuna. The blackened swordfish appears regularly as a dinner special and is a local favorite. Try the baked cod, which is coated in lightly seasoned bread crumbs and comes with a baked potato and fresh vegetables.

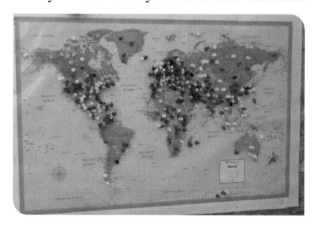

## COLD *AND* HOT LOBSTER ROLLS

The lobster rolls are big sellers at JT's. There is, of course, the traditional cold-style roll with mayo and spices served on a split-top bun, always popular with Bostonians and other northern New Englanders. A while back, one of Bud's friends from Connecticut suggested adding a hot, buttered lobster roll (the prevalent style in southern New England) to JT's menu. Bud tried it on an experimental basis, and in fairly short order, he had nearly doubled his lobster roll sales. (Now, *that's* a good friend!)

JT's takes pride in the heaping portions it serves up to its customers—typically two ounces more of the good stuff on the seafood dishes and one ounce more on the lobster rolls than the competition. The heaping amount of lobster in the hot and cold rolls cascades down the sides of the buns, making for an added bonus to nosh on after you've finished your sandwich. The fried

**JT'S** customers come from all around the world.

seafood dinners are fall-off-the-plate big, lightly and carefully fried in a blend of corn and canola oil, and delicately seasoned.

## LOBSTAH AND RIBS

You may partake of the traditional Cape Cod dinner of steamed lobster, corn on the cob, and a biscuit at JT's; you may also "supersize" your lobster et al to a shore dinner, which adds in a pound of steamed native clams and a bowl of flavorful broth for dipping.

One other dish to consider: JT's barbecued ribs. This is a bit unusual for a clam shack, but these baby back ribs with their special homemade sauce won't disappoint.

Don't forget about the ice cream. JT's has twenty different flavors between their soft and hard selections. They also have frozen yogurt, ice-cream sundaes, banana splits, and a limited amount of baked goods. There's a separate order window for all these goodies on the front of the building, right next to the tables and umbrellas.

So, if you're cruising 6A on the lookout for a good fried seafood stand or some cool, refreshing ice cream, don't be fooled by the dressy look of JT's. Come on in, in T-shirt, shorts, and flip-flops; place your order at the counter (and your pushpin in the wall); grab a seat; and enjoy some award-winning seafood in this clean, lively, and relaxed mid-Cape clam shack.

# Captain Frosty's Fish & Chips

**219 Main Street (Route 6A), Dennis, MA 02638 | (508) 385-8548 | www.captainfrosty.com**
**Open mid-April to late September**

There has always been a strong connection between ice cream and deep-fried seafood in the clam shack world, and that's definitely the case at Captain Frosty's of Dennis, Massachusetts.

Frosty's started out as an ice-cream place (as the name implies) in the 1950s, but it has become much more in succeeding years. Although ice cream is still an important part of the business that pulls in customers off of scenic Route 6A, it's the seafood that's the main draw these days.

## FROSTY'S BEGINNINGS

Just a quick glance at the building tells you that there's ice cream deeply embedded in the history of this shack. Captain Frosty's is housed in a classic ice-cream stand from the 1950s with glass on the front and sides and a sloping roof that rises from back to front like a pompadour. It's a striking edifice from the outside—and even more so from within.

## WOOD PANELING AND DUELING MENUS

While the exterior of Captain Frosty's shows off its glass fronts and chrome window frames, the interior is filled with warm, glowing, knotty-pine paneled wood in both the order area and the adjacent dining room. It feels more like northern Maine than Cape Cod. The indoor dining room was added on to the original structure by Mike and Pat Henderson, who transformed Frosty's from an ice-cream stand into a clam shack when they bought it in 1976.

The place still has a bit of a split personality, with separate order counters for food and ice cream and vintage hand-lettered, illuminated menus hanging over each—one featuring all the ice-cream treats and the other heralding the seafood-and-sandwiches lineup. There's an additional outdoor order window beneath a canopy on the front side of the building for ice-cream customers

**CAPTAIN** Frosty's sports the classic 1950s ice-cream-stand look.

**IN** case there's any doubt, this sign in the dining room reminds you just how fresh the fish is.

only. It can all be a bit confusing at first, but don't despair. Captain Frosty's cheerful, friendly staff will take good care of you, whether you're there for lunch, dinner, or dessert.

## A Little History

The Hendersons took over in the mid-1970s, and they expanded the kitchen and started cooking up fish and chips and other seafood dishes. They also built a tree-shaded patio in back to expand their seating capacity and dining options. Their son Matt, who now runs Captain Frosty's, recalls laying bricks for the patio one cold February in his youth, and he can still remember all too vividly the numbing sensation in his fingers. A second patio was added later on the front side of the shack, closer to the road; it too is a cozy, tree-shaded nook that's excellent for quiet and peaceful dining.

Mike and Pat rode the wave of clam shack popularity that began in the 1970s (when so many other clam shacks got started) and surged for the next twenty years or so, until people started becoming more health-conscious. The Hendersons then began expanding their menu to include not only deep-fried seafood and seafood rolls but also burgers, hot dogs, and eventually salads and a very tasty grilled salmon sandwich served with Dijon mayo on sourdough bread—a healthy choice by any standard.

## Great Seafood from Local Fishermen

Fish and chips and fried shellfish have remained the most popular mainstays at Frosty's; all are fried these days in pure, cholesterol-free canola oil. Like most shacks on the Cape, virtually all the seafood is from very local sources. The cod, haddock, and flounder come from Chatham, some ten miles distant, and any of the three fillet types may be had as the seafood half of the fish and chips platter. The scallops come from nearby day boats, so they're as fresh as can be. And the clams are from local beds, sweet, tender, and full of flavor when they're fried up in Frosty's ultra-clean deep fryers. Chewy, tender clam cakes and hand-cut onion rings make great deep-fried side dishes or just snacks for those who are less famished or not up to the task of a full-blown platter.

You may also get the scallops grilled on wooden skewers and served either with rice pilaf or as part of a meal-size salad. The lobster roll has won several local awards over the years. It's served cold with just a little bit of mayo. You may get the regular roll for $12 or so, or you may swing for the fences with the gigantic version, which features more than half a pound of lobster meat and costs around $20. Take your pick—either way you can't go wrong.

## Circle Back for Ice Cream

Whether you decide to dine at Frosty's or not, you should definitely pull in and partake of their old-time soft-serve ice cream, which has remained pretty much unchanged in its simplicity and rich flavor since the place opened over fifty years ago. The soft-serve comes in five flavors: vanilla, chocolate, twist (combo vanilla and chocolate), coffee, and yoberry (a tart-flavored frozen yogurt).

Frosty's has its own version of a DQ Blizzard called a Flurry, which may be had with various crushed cookies and candies mixed in. The sundaes are huge and come in hot fudge, butterscotch, strawberry, and pineapple. There's also a brownie hot fudge sundae and a Triple Swirl Banana Boat, Frosty's over-the-top version of a banana split. Frappes (aka milk shakes), ice-cream sodas, floats, and orange freezes round out the old-time ice-cream offerings at this classic roadside stand.

There may be crowds and long lines in the summer, and parking can be a challenge, as Frosty's has a relatively small parking lot and street parking is minimal on 6A. But this spot is such a wonderful throwback to shacks and stands of yesteryear that it's worth any wait you may have to endure. Show some patience with Captain Frosty's, and they'll repay you with some fine food and ice cream and a great place to sit in the shade on long summer days.

# Tony's Clam Shop

**861 Quincy Shore Drive, Quincy, MA 02170 | (617) 773-5090 | www.tonysclamshop.com**
**Open late March to mid-October**

Tony's Clam Shop isn't exactly on Cape Cod (not even close, really), but if you happen to be traveling between Boston and the Cape, or if you find yourself in the Quincy, Massachusetts, area just south of Boston, this is a place you should definitely check out.

Tony's sits right on the busy shoreline highway that cuts through the Wollaston Beach section of Quincy. Situated directly across the street from the locally popular Wollaston Beach, Tony's is an oasis among the adjacent

beachfront houses and apartments that line the road. The eatery has been providing deep-fried sustenance and plenty of other tasty food and drink to residents and beachgoers in this working class enclave for nearly fifty years.

## A CITY SHACK THROUGH AND THROUGH

Housed in a wooden, two-story, 1970s ski-lodge-condo-type building, Tony's is a focal point of social activity on the Wollaston Beach waterfront. This clam shack is more urban than most, and it is an integral part of the surrounding community.

Founder Tony Kandalaft and his wife Tilly started running Tony's out of the front of their house on this very spot in 1964. At one point in those early years, Tony had a buzzer installed by the order counter; he would press it when things got busy and he needed help. The buzzer sounded back in the living room of the Kandalaft home, summoning an often irritated Tilly, who preferred to focus her energies on tending to the couple's three children.

As business picked up and money started to

**GARY** Kandalaft, co-owner of Tony's Clam Shop.

roll in, the Kandalafts gradually transformed their home into a more commercial establishment. Bedrooms became storage areas, and closets disappeared as the shack's kitchen and other backroom operations grew. For

**TONY'S** is a city shack through and through.

a number of years, the Kandalafts continued to live in back of and above Tony's until they finally decamped to other housing nearby.

Tony is semi-retired at this point, and his three children—Gary, Roy, and Karen—have taken over day-to-day operations. It's a family-run business all the way. The teenaged third generation of Kandalafts has begun working at Tony's, and for a number of years, many of Gary, Roy, and Karen's cousins have also been on staff. Additionally, Tony's hires lots of people from the neighborhood to help out, particularly in the busy summer months, which further strengthens the shack's ties with the local community.

item on the menu. In fact, Tony's customers are so clam-crazy that over the years many started specifying the size and type of fried clams they prefer. This led the customer-conscious Kandalafts to start dividing up their daily clam purchases into three categories: big whole bellies, small whole bellies, and no bellies (not to be confused with clam strips). They even have buttons on their computerized cash registers to let the kitchen staff know which size clam each customer prefers. Now *that's* customer service.

The fried clams are lightly breaded and deep-fried to order, coming out crispy, sweet, and golden brown. They're Ipswich clams, so you know they're good. The fried fish fillets, scallops, clam strips, oysters, shrimp, lobster, and calamari receive the same TLC in the kitchen and are equally delightful à la carte or as platters with fries and coleslaw.

## THREE SIZES OF CLAMS

Tony's is a clam shack first and foremost, and Gary Kandalaft emphasizes that deep-fried whole-belly clams are by far the most popular

## WRAP AND ROLL

There's an amazing variety of wraps available at Tony's—everything from four different kinds of chicken to turkey, tuna, steak, and vegetarian.

Particularly popular is the BLT wrap. And in a nod to the Kandalafts' Middle Eastern heritage, there are hummus/tabouli and falafel wraps.

The lobster roll is a sight to behold: half a pound of cold lobster salad loaded onto a split-top, toasted, buttered bun that's almost impossible to find beneath the mound of lobster meat. There are also rolls for fried clams, clam strips, scallops, shrimp, oysters, and calamari. All come in the form of baskets with french fries on the side.

Numerous other sandwiches are available from the grill and deli, including burgers, hot dogs, grilled cheese, and subs.

There has always been a patio in front of Tony's, offering a great view of the beach across the street and an inspiring backdrop of the Boston skyline in the distance. Over the years, the patio has grown, and it's now covered with numerous classy-looking tables, chairs, and umbrellas that lend a big-city, café-type atmosphere to the front of the place. It's a great spot for people-watching, as beachgoers and locals parade in front of Tony's day and night.

Indoors, across from the lengthy order counter, are a bunch of tables enclosed within a greenhouse-like glass front on the building. It

**TONY'S** has something unique in the world of clam shacks—a view of a big-city skyline.

gives you the opportunity to enjoy the sunshine yet dine in air-conditioned comfort, if you wish.

Regardless of where you choose to sit, you don't need to worry about missing the call when your food is ready. Tony's gives each customer a small, plastic, lobster-shaped buzzer that shakes, flashes, and hums when your order is ready to be picked up. So, go forth, find a dining spot to your liking, and wait for that lobster to come to life, letting you know that your sweet reward awaits you at the counter.

Speaking of sweet rewards, there's an ice-cream stand next to the order counter that displays sixteen different flavors of hard-packed ice cream. There's not much that Tony's doesn't have to help make your day just a little bit better, so take a cruise down to Wollaston Beach and enjoy the finest that Tony's and Quincy have to offer.

## Middle Eastern Delights at Tony's

The Kandalaft clan is of mixed Syrian and Lebanese ancestry, and they have brought some of their native cuisine to this fine dining spot on the shores of Quincy Bay. In addition to the falafel, hummus, and tabouli wraps, you may enjoy a hummus plate, tabouli salad, a falafel plate, or the kafta plate with beef, onions, parsley, and five different types of peppers.

Perhaps the tastiest and most popular Middle Eastern dish on the menu is the grilled chicken kebabs. These nicely seasoned skewers of marinated chicken breast are served with pita bread and a Greek salad. Neighborhood devotees wait all winter long for Tony's to reopen in the spring, when there's a small mob of kebab-deprived customers lining up on opening day to get their reaffirming kebab fix.

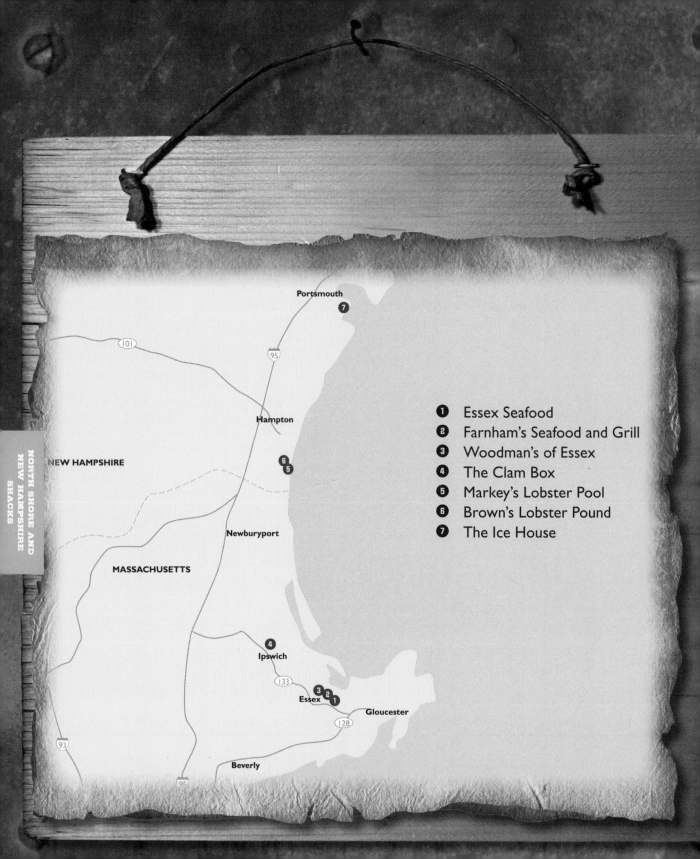

Portsmouth

**7**

101

95

Hampton

NEW HAMPSHIRE

**6**
**5**

Newburyport

MASSACHUSETTS

**4**

Ipswich

133

**3** **2** **1**

Essex

Gloucester

128

93

Beverly

95

**1** Essex Seafood
**2** Farnham's Seafood and Grill
**3** Woodman's of Essex
**4** The Clam Box
**5** Markey's Lobster Pool
**6** Brown's Lobster Pound
**7** The Ice House

# NORTH SHORE AND NEW HAMPSHIRE SHACKS

**The North Shore of Massachusetts, which** begins with Cape Ann just north and east of Boston and extends to the state's northern border, includes the lovely seaside towns of Essex and Ipswich and the famous historical fishing towns of Gloucester and Rockport. This part of Massachusetts is the Garden of Eden when it comes to clam shacks—the place where the fried clam is said to have been invented and home to a handful of the oldest and most famous clam shacks in all of New England. Many are located on Route 133, dubbed the "Clam Highway," and in a span of a leisurely day or two, you may visit all of them and sample the various seafood specialties of each.

The Cape Ann area also boasts some of the finest soft-shell clam beds in the world. They are found in and among the vast stretch of tidal marshlands and estuaries that begin in Cape Ann and extend northward almost to Maine.

New Hampshire's shacks have their own charm, two of them being just over the Massachusetts border and across the road from one another in friendly competition, and a third shack further up the coast and just outside the old seafaring city of Portsmouth.

There's a lot of character and variety in this hallowed section of the clam shack world, and some of the best fried clams on the face of the earth.

# J. T. Farnham's Seafood and Grill

**88 Eastern Avenue, Essex, MA 01929 | (978) 768-6643 | Open early March to late November**

While motoring up Route 133 into Essex from Gloucester, you'll find one of the finest and most heralded clam shacks in all of New England: J. T. Farnham's Seafood and Grill. Some consider Farnham's the best in the land; others contend nearby Woodman's is best, while still others vote for the Clam Box some five miles north on Route 133 in Ipswich. Regardless of how you cast your vote, you're in major-league fried-clam country here, and no matter which of these establishments you choose to patronize, you really can't go wrong.

**J. T.** Farnham's classic, classy road sign.

|||||| FARNHAM'S LINEAGE ||||||

Farnham's has been in existence for nearly seventy years, though it originally opened under a different name. John "Shine" Wilson got things going when he opened a restaurant where Farnham's currently stands in 1941; he sold his eatery three years later to Joe and Matilda Farnham. Their son Joe Farnham Jr. eventually took over and ran Farnham's with his wife, Janice, until 1994. That's when current owners Joseph and Terry Cellucci bought it and began rebuilding the restaurant from the inside out.

Farnham's already had a reputation for fine deep-fried clams and other seafood when Joseph and Terry took over, so they inherited (and still retain) a passionately loyal local customer base that helps keep the business running smoothly throughout its nine-month-long season. Wedged between Route 133 and the salt marsh in back, Farnham's looks a bit like an elongated, gray-shingled house with a small parking lot and a string of picnic tables on the side and in back. There are three separate doors on the front of the building, but don't be confused. The one in the middle of the building will get you where you want to go: straight to the order counter and the fine food served within.

**DEEP-FRIED** clams and seafood chowder are two of the highlights at Farnham's.

## A 1990s MAKEOVER

The interior of Farnham's has a warm, homey feel to it—sort of like a country diner. There are several varnished wooden booths lining a side wall and a handful of free-standing tables in the middle of the room. If it's available, try to grab the table that's positioned in front of the picture window at the rear of the dining room. It has a gorgeous view of the salt marsh in back that stretches all the way to the sea. At high tide, boaters can make their way by water to Farnham's, tie up, and go in for a meal. A sea plane even landed out back once, depositing hungry customers at Farnham's back door.

When Joseph and Terri bought the place, neither of them had any real experience in the restaurant business. Joseph had been employed in the high-tech sector, and Terri was quite busy at the time raising the couple's two young daughters. They were driving by Farnham's one day in 1994 when they noticed a blown-over FOR SALE sign next to the building. They inquired within, and before long, they worked out a deal with the Farnhams and took possession of the restaurant, which was starting to slide into disrepair.

The Celluccis immediately started spiffing the place up, refurbishing the interior, and then expanding the back of the building by ten feet or so to allow a little more space for the dining area and to enlarge the cramped kitchen. They got all-new food service equipment, including a new six-burner gas stove and several new deep fryers. The Farnhams had been using a hand-cranked meat grinder to mash up onions for their chowders, and the Celluccis replaced it with an electric food processor. All through the upgrade process, they continued serving up the clams and other seafood that had made Farnham's locally famous.

## Farnham's Famous Crab Cakes

Although best known for their out-of-this-world fried clams, the Farnham's crab cakes are a hidden gem on their menu. Here is Terry Cellucci's recipe, for your enjoyment at home:

INGREDIENTS

2  red bell peppers, chopped

½  onion, minced

2  pounds crabmeat (fresh if available, canned if not)

2  eggs, beaten

   Juice from ½ lemon

1  tablespoon Worcestershire sauce

1  tablespoon Old Bay spice

1  tablespoon paprika

1  tablespoon parsley

1  teaspoon salt

½  teaspoon black pepper

1  cup bread crumbs

1  cup cracker crumbs

Add the diced red bell pepper and onion to the crabmeat. Beat the eggs, lemon, and Worcestershire sauce together, then add to the crab mixture. Add all the spices and mix thoroughly. Add bread crumbs and cracker crumbs, and mix well. Form into cakes (⅓ cup mixture per cake). Deep-fry or sauté cakes until evenly cooked. Yields eighteen crab cakes. Serve with lemon, hot sauce, and/or tartar sauce.

Among fried clam aficionados, debates rage constantly over who serves the best ones on the Clam Highway. The Food Network's *Food Feuds* pitted Farnham's fried clams against those from the vaunted Woodman's of Essex in 2010, and Farnham's prevailed. They have the trophy to prove it and proudly display it next to the cash register.

There are a few things about the fried clams served in this part of the world that set them apart from nearly all others. For starters, some sort of animal fat is used in the frying process. At Farnham's, the oil in the fryer is a mixture of animal fat (they won't say what kind) and vegetable oil. This makes a huge difference in the flavor, and Farnham's clams score high on the flavor scale. The fried whole bellies are tender, flaky with light breading, chewy, and crunchy all at the same time—quite a unique and unforgettable experience. The oil at Farnham's is changed daily and more frequently during the busy summer season.

The other mark of distinction with Farnham's clams is that they are locally sourced from the Ipswich Shellfish Company and Ipswich Maritime. These companies harvest their clams (when conditions permit) right in the Ipswich/Essex area, which has some of the best clam beds in the world. So, the product is super fresh, and the Celluccis (like their nearby competitors) are very picky about the clams they'll take from their suppliers.

There are a few different ways to enjoy these deep-fried gems. You may buy them by the box (half-pint, pint, or quart); you may get them as part of a dinner plate, which comes with french fries, onion rings, and coleslaw (pick two); or as a "boat," served with fries only. No matter which one you choose, you really can't go wrong.

## CHOWDER CHOICES

The other truly outstanding item at Farnham's is the chowder—actually, there are four kinds. The New England clam chowder is milky, rich with flavor, and chock-full of minced clam meat and perfectly cooked chunks of potato. The haddock chowder is much the same, substituting bite-size bits of haddock for clams. For the more adventurous, there's a Manhattan spicy scallop chowder, which is a red chowder containing plump, whole sea scallops and bits of potato simmered a spicy broth. Perhaps the best of them all is what Farnham's immodestly calls "The Best Seafood Chowder." This is a light-brothed white chowder with reddish streaks of tomato through it and copious amounts of clams, haddock, shrimp, sea scallops, and chunks of lobster meat. The seafood chowder isn't cheap, but it's oh-so-worth it.

## THREE DINING OPTIONS

You've got a few choices on where to dine when at Farnham's. Regardless of which one you choose, though, you have to step up to the counter (or the outside order window) and place your order, as no server will visit your table to take it. Once you've done so, here are your options:

○ **The counter.** There's a relatively short one with several chair-backed stools stretching out from the cash register.

○ **The dining room.** This is a particularly nice choice, especially in cool or inclement weather, as the small room is cozy and inviting.

○ **The picnic tables.** Nothing beats eating out here in warm, sunny weather. You've got a great view of the salt marsh before you and of the oft-photographed and painted Andrew Wyeth-esque house just across the marsh from the parking lot and picnic tables.

If you've already filled up on victuals at one of the other fine establishments on the Clam Highway, you should still swing by Farnham's and score a half-pint of fried clams, if for no other reason than to compare them to the others you've just had and perhaps to make your own *Food Feud*-type determination of who makes the best fried bivalves in the land.

# A David Among Goliaths

**Essex Seafood | 143 Eastern Avenue, Essex, MA 01929 | (978) 768-7233 | www.essexseafood.com**

If you blink, you may miss this place. It's tucked behind a large house on Route 133 on the left-hand side of the road as you travel over the town border from Gloucester into Essex. Its simple signage—ESSEX SEAFOOD/OPEN YEAR-ROUND—is your only clue that it's there and that it's open for business when many the area's other clam shacks of greater size and distinction have shut down for the season.

Owned by Howie and Debbie Lane, this little gem of a shack holds its own quite nicely in the august company of such nearby titans as Farnham's, Woodman's, and the Clam Box. It's got a seafood market that's primarily a lobster pound, where you may purchase live lobsters or have them cooked for take-home or for dining out back at the outdoor picnic tables.

Next to the market and in the same building is a small, L-shaped diner-type clam shack. The order counter is to your right as you enter, and all the offerings are listed on a dry-erase board next to the window. Across from the counter and wrapping around the back is a small, cozy, pine-paneled dining room filled with nautical paraphernalia and about a dozen booths. Essex Seafood shucks their own clams on the premises—a rarity these days—so you can expect the freshest of fried clams and a very tasty clam chowder. The clam cakes are also extraordinary—a bit greasy but full of clammy flavor and a nice pairing with a cup of chowder any time of day.

Boiled lobster is probably the most popular dish here, but all the fried seafood definitely satisfies, also. Though this place may seem to exist only to handle the overflow from the more famous shacks down the road, Essex Seafood can more than hold its own in the face of such competition. The fact that the locals love it and keep it going year-round is testament to its quality and its tenacity in the cutthroat competitive local market known as the Clam Highway.

**THE** diminutive yet mighty Essex Seafood.

# Woodman's of Essex

121 Main Street, Essex, MA 01929 | (978) 768-2559 | www.woodmans.com | Open year-round

For all the hoopla surrounding what is likely the world's most famous clam shack (and certainly one of the best), you might expect it to be some sort of super-slick, modern, steel-and-chrome colossus gleaming from the roadside, with klieg lights criss-crossing the sky at night, attracting hungry seafood fans like moths to a flame. Yet what you find when you pull up to Woodman's on Route 133 in Essex is a jumble of somewhat ramshackle buildings of various architectural styles, sizes, and vintages. None of them seem to match, and the only thing they have in common are the signs letting you know that, yes, you've arrived at Woodman's of Essex, the place where it all started.

Like the Lincoln Memorial, the Baseball Hall of Fame, and other great shrines around the country, all lovers of deep-fried clams should make a pilgrimage to this spot where, on July 3, 1916, Lawrence "Chubby" Woodman is said to have taken some of his freshly shucked clams and immersed them in a vat of hot cooking oil, essentially inventing what we know today as the fried clam.

## THE LAY OF THE LAND

Woodman's is situated between a couple of bends in the Essex River as the stream meanders its way through the Great Salt Marsh on its way to the sea. In back of Woodman's is a large parking lot and a bunch of picnic tables on a patch of elevated land that overlooks the marshy upstream portion of the river. It's a great place to enjoy your Woodman's repast on a nice day. You may view canoes, small motorboats, and kayaks plying the river, and the surrounding marsh is often full of avian life (including, sometimes—diner beware—hungry seagulls).

**WOODMAN'S** ever-busy order counter.

Walking back through the parking lot toward the Woodman's compound of buildings on Route 133, you'll first encounter a seasonal ice-cream stand of relatively recent vintage and a gift shop that's filled with all sorts of Woodman's and other local paraphernalia. Proceed on to Woodman's proper, which is housed in a vintage two-story shingled building facing directly on to Route 133. A raw bar occupies the second floor in back.

## The Invention of the Fried Clam

Legend has it that the fried clam was invented in Essex, Massachusetts, at a little roadside stand by Lawrence "Chubby" Woodman and his wife, Bessie, on July 3, 1916. Here's how the story goes:

In 1914, Chubby and Bessie opened a roadside concession stand on Main Street (Route 133) in Essex, selling groceries, fresh clams dug by Chubby himself on the local flats, and homemade potato chips that he fried up in the couple's large, lard-laden frying pot. Business was slow for the first year or two, until one momentous day in the summer of 1916.

On July 3, Chubby was chatting with a local fisherman in front of the store, bemoaning the slow pace of business on the eve of the town's Fourth of July celebration. The fisherman jokingly suggested that Chubby try frying up some clams in the pot, which at first sounded like lunacy. But the more Chubby thought about it, the more he thought that it might be worth a try. It could create a new way for him to sell his fresh clams to all the hungry passersby.

So, like a couple of roadside recipe testers, Chubby and Bessie gave it a try. After a bit of experimentation with battering and coating, they offered a batch of golden fried clams to some locals, who gobbled them up and immediately demanded more. The Woodmans were clearly on to something. The next day, they offered their fried clams at Essex's Fourth of July parade. The response was immediate and enduring.

On the back side of their wedding certificate, Chubby and Bessie wrote down what they considered to be important events in their family life. Among the entries: "We fried the first fried clam—in the town of Essex, July 3, 1916."

**LAWRENCE** "Chubby" Woodman.

The real action, however, begins on the street in front of Woodman's. There's a lobster stand where you pick out your own among the numerous ones of various sizes alive and iced down on a stainless steel table. Make your selection, then wait for it to be cooked on the spot in a large outdoor cauldron and handed over to you for feasting. It's a cheerfully casual, almost hands-on way to get your lobster, and the fact that it's outdoors makes your crimson crustacean taste all the more fresh when you step inside Woodman's to find a booth or return out back to the picnic tables for your feast.

Right next to the lobster stand is the main entrance to Woodman's, where you go to place your deep-fried seafood order. It won't be hard to find, as there's usually a long line of hungry customers snaking out the door and down the street, especially in the summertime. Queue up and be patient. All good things are worth waiting for.

## The Main Show

Woodman's is quite a production, with its large and lucrative catering and mail order businesses, its banquet hall, the raw bar, ice-cream stand, and airy outdoor lobstertorium. But the main show here is the deep-fried seafood, most notably the clams that made Woodman's famous, and dining in the rough in Woodman's

**PICK** your own live lobster out front at Woodman's.

rustic, expansive indoor dining room on the first floor is the best way to enjoy it.

Once you've made it through the front door and the order counter is in sight (hallelujah!), fix your gaze on the chalkboard menu suspended above the counter. The menu's simplicity is striking: clams, strips, sea scallops, shrimp, and haddock are the main choices from the deep fryer. A generously portioned cold lobster roll and deep-fried lobster tail are other standouts. By far the best side dish is the batter-dipped onion rings, virtually the only battered item on the menu. They're crispy, crunchy, and oh so sweet. Fries are also outstanding, as are the homemade coleslaw, flavorful clam cakes, and creamy, rich New England–style clam chowder.

## What Makes Their Clams So Good?

There seem to be two main things that set Woodman's clams apart from virtually all others. First, the shack hasn't wavered from Tubby's initial method of frying them in lard. This, of course, isn't great for your cholesterol count, but these clams score off the chart on the flavor scale. Woodman's uses a quick milk wash, followed by a thorough coating in a bin filled with corn flour, which guarantees a light, flavorful, crispy, golden brown crunch of heavenly flavor in each whole-bellied bite.

Second, all of Woodman's clams are very carefully sourced from the nearby flats. The fried whole bellies tend to be on the smaller side, as Woodman's (and many other establishments) believe them to be the most flavorful. And, given the sheer volume that Woodman's procures, they can afford to be picky and accept only the best from their suppliers.

Similar care is taken in sourcing the lobsters, haddock, sea scallops, and jumbo shrimp. You may have any of these delights as part of a fried plate (includes fries *and* onion rings) or à la carte in half-pint, pint, and quart boxes.

**A** box of deep-fried heaven at Woodman's.

## THE WOODMAN'S DINING EXPERIENCE

Once you've placed your order, go around the corner into the dining area, where you'll find the pickup window, and wait for your number to be called. (You'll pass by a strategically placed service bar between the order and pickup areas; feel free to grab a beverage while you wait.) Dinners and most other food orders come heaped on paper plates that are set inside the bottom halves of cardboard Miller beer case holders, which help make transporting your order to your booth or table much easier.

Woodman's indoor dining rooms are charming, cozy, and filled with low-slung wooden booths, which helps create a festive atmosphere. There are a couple of public beaches near Woodman's and in summertime you'll find lots of fellow diners in bathing suits and sandals.

Once you've enjoyed your meal, feel free to stroll the grounds, check out the gift shop, grab an ice-cream cone, or poke your head into any of the busy backroom operations at this clam shack mecca. You're on hallowed ground here, so soak it all up and vow to come back just as soon as possible because this is as authentic as clam shacks get.

**A** box of deep-fried heaven at Woodman's.

# The Clam Box

**246 High Street, Ipswich, MA 01938 | (978) 356-9707 | Open mid-February to mid-December**

When fried clam lovers first set their eyes upon the Clam Box of Ipswich, Massachusetts, it's like *The Wizard of Oz*'s Dorothy and her friends emerging from the dark forest and gazing upon the glorious City of Oz for the first time. As you come around a bend in Route 133 (also known as the Clam Highway), there it is, standing tall and proud by the side of the road, shaped like an old-fashioned, two-story-tall, open-topped clam box, daring you to drive by without stopping.

Along with Woodman's and Farnham's down the road in Essex, the Clam Box is one of the titans of the New England clam shack scene. This place is legendary, and people travel great distances to experience it. Jane and Michael Stern of *Road Food* fame have brought busloads of people here on numerous occasions to sample firsthand the Clam Box's deep-fried fare. There's almost always a line spilling out of the door and winding back into the expansive parking lot; it's a line well worth joining, though, as these clams may very well be the best you can get anywhere.

## THE ORIGINS OF "THE BOX"

The Clam Box sits in what is today a purely residential neighborhood full of houses and lawns, with nary another commercial enterprise in sight.

How did this unusual edifice come to be? Back in 1935, a man named Dick Greenleaf built the Clam Box for his wife so she could run a food stand as a hobby. The Greenleafs soon tired of the novelty and sold the business to a Mr. Sperling, who ran it for a few decades and in turn sold the Clam Box to Skip Atwood in the 1970s. Skip added the dining room and the

**THE** one-of-a-kind Clam Box façade pretty much says it all.

enclosed vestibule over the order and pickup windows. This allowed him to extend the Clam Box's season with an earlier opening date in the spring and a later closing date in the fall.

## THE CHICKIE FACTOR

Come the mid-1980s, Atwood tired of the business, letting it get a little ragged around the edges, and he put it up for sale. Ipswich native Marina "Chickie" Aggelakis took an interest in the unusual eatery, bought it from Atwood, and immediately set about fixing the place up and getting it running properly once again.

Chickie was no stranger to the restaurant business. Her father founded the Agawam Diner, a vintage polished-chrome eatery on U.S. Route 1 in nearby Rowley. She also worked in other local restaurants around Ipswich in her teens and twenties.

Chickie seems to have been born to own the Clam Box. She has lovingly preserved it as the amazing icon that it is, with its distinctive gray shingled exterior and colorful red-and-white awnings and signage. She expanded the parking lot in back and added a deck with several picnic tables under some shade trees at the rear of the property for outdoor dining. She also made significant improvements to the kitchen over time, to accommodate the steadily increasing amount of business the Clam Box was doing. The lines

started forming outside the door and in the parking lot only after Chickie took the helm.

## THE CLAM BOX EXPERIENCE

The best way to enjoy the Clam Box to its fullest is to come with a big appetite, an open heart, and a little bit of patience. Even in the off-season, there's usually a line to get into the vestibule where you place your order. There are a couple of wrought-iron benches to sit on out front as you near the door, but with any luck, you'll be up and out of them quickly as the line moves steadily forward.

Once you've reached the inner sanctum, there's a menu posted over the order windows for your perusal. At this point, you also get a peek into the bustling kitchen, where half a dozen or more youthful workers scurry about, custom-preparing each order. It's a case study in efficiency, as Chickie has every work station in the kitchen finely tuned to specific duties.

Like at most top clam shacks, the menu at the Clam Box is quite simple: On the seafood side, there are deep-fried whole-belly clams, clam strips, scallops, shrimp, haddock, oysters, and calamari to choose from. You may get each à la carte in small or large boxes, or as part of a plate (served with fries, onion rings, or coleslaw—pick two) or a mini-meal (pick one).

The deep-fried whole-belly clams cannot

be recommended highly enough. These native clams are hand-picked and inspected by Chickie herself each morning when suppliers arrive with the day's fresh catch. Chickie demands uniformity in size and firmness, and it shows in the consistently outstanding finished product.

## WHAT MAKES THEM SO GOOD?

Once the clams pass inspection, each order is carefully measured, then dipped into a wash of evaporated milk. Next comes a thorough hand-kneading in a stainless steel tub containing three parts corn flour to one part white pastry flour. The kneading process ensures uniform, thorough coverage of each clam, and any excess flour is then shaken off.

Deep-frying is a two-step process. First, the clams are dropped for a few seconds into a deep fryer for a "washing," where any excess flour that hasn't adhered to the clams is cooked away. Then the clams are placed in a second fryer where the actual cooking occurs. The end result is a deep-fried clam belly that is succulently sweet, crunchy, and loaded with fresh clam flavor. Most of the other deep-fried seafood items receive the same exacting process from the Clam Box's experienced cook staff. When you bite into your first Clam Box fried clam, you immediately sense the difference between these fried clams and pretty much all the others.

**THE** Clam Box's bustling kitchen, where some of New England's best prepared seafood comes from.

There are a couple of other things the Clam Box does to insure a great deep-fried seafood experience. First, the oil is a mixture of beef fat and vegetable oil, a blend similar to other operations on the Clam Highway. Chickie prefers beef to pork in her oil mixture for its flavor and lack of aftertaste.

Second, all the cooking oil at the Clam Box is changed *twice* daily, even in the shoulder seasons when business is slower. Chickie is a strong believer in the necessity of clean cooking oil throughout the day, and she goes to great effort and expense to deliver a consistently delicious product. The Clam Box starts with a fresh batch of oil mixture when they open around 11 a.m., and they replace it at 2:30 p.m. each day. There are signs outside the front door and by the order window thanking customers for their patience during the fifteen-minute oil-change hiatus in mid-afternoon. Though it may increase your wait time for your food, you'll be rewarded with some really tasty, greaseless, lip-smacking fried seafood when the cooking recommences.

## THE BEST OF THE REST

The lobster roll at the Clam Box is outstanding. It's a cold roll chock-full of freshly picked meat, served on a toasted split-top bun. You can also

### Chickie's Clam Box Tartar Sauce

Chickie Aggelakis will be the first to admit that her recipe for tartar sauce isn't rocket science; instead, it's a simple, handmade concoction that yields a heavenly, creamy, tangy sauce that goes well on any seafood (deep-fried or otherwise). Here it is:

7 ounces mayonnaise

4 ounces sweet (*not dill*) relish

1½ ounces ground-up heart of onion (the sweet part that's left after removing the onion rings for frying)

Mix ingredients in a bowl. Chill. Serve.

count on the burgers and hot dogs to be grilled just right and, for a few dollars more, they may be had with fries and homemade coleslaw.

Speaking of slaw, Chickie has a secret recipe for hers, and her kitchen staff whips up fresh batches throughout the day, along with homemade tartar sauce. And the hand-cut onion rings are fried in similarly fresh cooking oil, guaranteeing a sweet, crispy crunchiness.

## YOUR SWEET REWARD

Once you've picked up your order at the take-out window, you need to find a place to sit. There's a cute little indoor dining room adjacent to the take-out window that's filled with nautical décor, booths, and tables. Or you may exit the building and head to the rear of the parking lot where you'll find several picnic tables on a deck. Outdoors is the way to go in good weather, but you'll have to navigate your way through the sometimes busy parking lot with your tray in hand in order to get there.

The best clam shacks are those that have owners who are on the job constantly, watching over every aspect of their operation, as hungry— then satisfied—customers come and go. Chickie Aggelakis is a cheerful permanent fixture at the Clam Box of Ipswich, watching over her audacious red-and-white clam shack empire, and for that we should all be extremely grateful.

# Markey's Lobster Pool

**420 Route 286, Seabrook, NH 03874 | (603) 474-2851 | Open year-round**

When heading east on Route 286 toward the Seabrook oceanfront in southeastern New Hampshire, about a quarter mile before hitting the coastal road, you'll come across twin mammoth shacks straddling the highway: Markey's Lobster Pool and directly across the street, Brown's Lobster Pound. These two roadside mega-shacks face each other in friendly competition, vying for customers going to and from the nearby beaches, yet there seem to be plenty

more than enough hungry patrons to go around, as the long lines in front of each establishment on summer days attest. When you approach the twin shacks, Markey's will be on your right, so let's go there first.

## HOW MARKEY'S CAME TO BE

Markey's is actually the Johnny-come-lately in the cross-street rivalry, as Brown's was founded in the early 1950s, and Markey's opened some twenty years later. Owner Tom Markey and his parents got things going in 1972, shortly after Tom was discharged from the armed services. They began their seafood stand modestly in a smallish, one-story building and slowly grew the business (and the building) over time.

Markey's is currently housed in a low, flat, expansive, whitewashed structure abutting the Blackwater River, a broad tidal stream that rises and falls a couple of times each day just off Markey's back-deck dining area. At certain times of day, you seem to be almost at eye level with the water, and at others, the river flows placidly by, several feet below the back side of the restaurant. Tom says that when a big storm

**MARKEY'S** famed lobster cooker can boil up to 100 lobsters at a time.

hits the southern New Hampshire coast, portions of Markey's, including the parking lot in front, disappear briefly under water. (Thankfully, this doesn't happen often.)

The expansive interior, with its whitewashed walls and well-worn indoor/outdoor carpeting, has a bit of a rec room feel to it, except that it's much more massive and sprawling. The combined seating capacity for both the dining room and the outdoor deck is 375 persons, so you know that Markey's can really pack 'em in when things heat up in the summertime.

As for relations with the Browns across the street, Markey says they get along great, especially since both establishments stay so busy during the summer months. The only real difference he sees between the two is that you may order beer and wine at Markey's while Brown's is BYO. Take your choice.

**A** tray full of Markey's finest.

## BOILED LOBSTERS AND MUCH MORE

Once you advance far enough in the often lengthy line and enter the front door of Markey's, you find yourself face to face with several cold-water lobster tanks and a large, steaming, cube-shaped stainless-steel lobster cooker. It's attended by two or three busy cooks lowering lobsters in small nets into the hot water for a quick scalding. It's quite a sight to behold the number of lobsters being dunked in the cooker on busy summer days; each netted crustacean is tethered to a block of wood along the rim of the pound for quick and easy identification and removal when cooked. The massive, gas-fired lobster cooker can handle up to 100 lobsters at a time, a typical number needed for large clam bakes, which Markey's caters on a regular basis. Daily lobster prices are displayed on a chalk board next to the pound, and they're more than reasonable.

If lobster isn't going to be your thing that day, turn to the left and you'll find yourself in line at the order counter for a wide variety of deep-fried seafood, side orders, chowders, and grilled sandwiches.

Although Markey's prides itself on its brisk and lively lobster business, the deep fryers here yield up a huge amount of tasty treats. People come from miles around for the fried clams and scallops, and for the fried haddock, which is served both as a sandwich on a bun and as part of a massive dinner plate that includes fries and coleslaw. You may also get fried lobster, shrimp, oysters, clam cakes, and fried chicken à la carte or with fries and slaw.

The onion rings and clam cakes are two more highlights from the deep fryers; both go great with a cup of Markey's homemade, creamy New England–style clam chowder.

Two other nice features are the recently installed raw bar, with clams and oysters on the half shell, which sits next to the lobster area, and a dedicated steamer stand in the main dining room, where you may order up steamed clams or mussels by the pound and enjoy them with broth and butter. The steamer stand also serves as the bar for procuring beer and wine.

The best way to enjoy Markey's is to snag your food inside, then head for the covered deck in back, where you may gaze out on the river and surrounding marsh grass. It's quiet back here, away from the street and the crowds up front, and it's especially nice at sunset. On a warm summer day with a bit of a breeze blowing and a tray of freshly cooked seafood in front of you, it's pretty much guaranteed you won't want to leave Markey's any time soon.

**MARKEY'S** outdoor deck hugs the tidal Blackwater River.

# Brown's Lobster Pound

**407 Route 286, Seabrook, NH 03874 | (603) 474-3331 | www.brownslobsterpound.com | Open year-round**

Right across the street from Markey's is the original shack on this stretch of the Blackwater River—Brown's Lobster Pound, which dates back nearly sixty years to 1952, when Hollis Brown and his business partner converted their lobster pound into a full-fledged seafood shack. With its distinctive gold, brown, and red building and signs, there's no confusing Brown's with the blue-and-white Markey's across the street.

## How Brown's Got Started

After being laid off from his job as a foreman in a shoe factory in the mid-1940s, Hollis Brown and a friend began hauling lobsters from Maine down to southern New Hampshire and northeastern Massachusetts and selling them wholesale to grocery stores and restaurants. They opened their own lobster pound in Hampton, New Hampshire, in the late 1940s, then moved to Brown's current location in Seabrook

**THERE'S** lots of bonhomie in Brown's spacious dining hall.

to a spot where the adjacent tidal waters of the Blackwater River were better for their lobsters. After a couple of years as a lobsters-only operation, they decided to add fried seafood to the menu and started serving up meals to patrons who would pull in and dine in the rough at several picnic tables scattered around the grounds. In the mid-1950s, Hollis bought out his partner, and Brown's as we know it was off and running.

Hollis's son Bruce has been involved with the business almost from the beginning, working at the lobster pound while still in high school. Upon graduating in 1955, Bruce came to work for Brown's full time. He took over the business from his parents, who retired in 1972, and he has been running it ever since. Two of Bruce's sons and four of his grandchildren are heavily involved in the management and operations of Brown's these days, making the shack a rare fourth-generation family-business success story.

## Built with Loving Care

As business increased back in the 1960s, so did Brown's. Hollis was a skilled woodworker, and over time, he added on to the original shack with an expansive wooden dining room and an open-air deck overhanging the river. The current dining hall almost has the feel of a logging camp mess hall, with its post-and-beam construction and forty or so handcrafted wooden booths, all made by Hollis in the off-seasons.

Nowadays, there are four basic parts to Brown's: the original shack, which houses the expanded kitchen and the fried seafood order window; the adjacent lobster pound with its cold-water tanks and its massive cooker; the wooden dining hall; and the deck on the west end overhanging the river. The wooden floor in the dining hall is repainted every year before the busy season begins, as the river occasionally floods the room and Brown's parking lot at high tide on stormy days. In fact, there are a couple of portholes in the dining room floor that are opened to drain out overflow when the need arises.

## Pick Your Own Lobster

One of the most enjoyable things to do at Brown's is to wander among the cold-water tanks in search of the lobster that will be your meal that day. The helpful staff will snag whichever crustacean looks good to you, then net it, give you a small wooden paddle with a number branded on it for identification, and pop your lobster into the gas-fired cooking vat. When it's reddened and ready several minutes later, the staff will crack the shells with a mallet and serve it up for you on a tray with drawn butter.

Brown's got started by hauling lobsters from Maine, and that's still where most of their catch comes from. Steamed clams, also from Maine, are another big draw at Brown's and are served up by the pound when in season.

## DOUBLE-WASH FRIED SEAFOOD

Back in the busy kitchen at Brown's, hundreds of pounds of fresh seafood are fried up nearly every day in the summertime. The Browns have a unique way of preparing their fish and shellfish for frying. First, they immerse the raw seafood in an egg wash with a bit of milk mixed in, then they dredge it in flour. Then it's back to the egg wash for a second dunking, followed by a visit to the cracker crumb vat. The end result is deep-fried seafood that's thoroughly coated, rich in flavor, and crunchy in texture. It's a lot of work for each cooked-to-order batch, but

**THIS** customer's T-shirt makes his allegiance known when dining in southern New Hampshire.

customers certainly appreciate it, and they keep coming back for more.

The clams and scallops at Brown's also come from Maine on a daily basis and are nearly as popular as the lobster and steamers. The fish fillet is haddock, and the shrimp hail from the Gulf of Mexico. Among the chowders, the fish chowder is the best, made fresh daily from portions of the haddock fillets. The baked lobster pie is an interesting alternative to the deep-fried platters, as it features generous chunks of lobster meat in a homemade pie crust.

Given the massive amounts of lobster cooked here daily, it goes without saying that the cold lobster salad roll is as fresh as can be. The meat is hand-picked by the kitchen staff throughout the day and is mixed with a little bit of mayo and served on a bed of lettuce tucked inside a top-split bun.

Keep this place in mind if you happen to be on your way to or from Maine, as it's only a few minutes east of I-95. It's also a great day trip from Boston or anywhere else in northeastern Massachusetts. Together with Markey's across the street, Brown's does southern New Hampshire proud with a fine tradition of no-muss, no-fuss seafood in a casual setting on the banks of the mercurial yet benign Blackwater River.

# The Ice House

112 Wentworth Road, Rye, NH 03870 | (603) 431-3086 | www.theicehouserestaurant.com
**Open mid-April to late October**

Just south and east of historic Portsmouth, New Hampshire, is the pretty little town of Rye, home of the Ice House, a shack on a quiet residential street in a very nice corner of the New Hampshire coast. This clam shack is a tough one to find, as you have to navigate down a number of twisting, curving streets in order to reach it. But it's a welcome, family-oriented respite from the bustle of Portsmouth and the fast food joints along Route 1 and I-95, so it's well worth the detour and the search that it takes to get there.

## TUGBOAT ROOTS

The Ice House has been in business a little over thirty years, but there has been an eatery of one sort or another at the same spot for more than half a century. A place called Bartlett's first popped up here in 1952, and it stayed in business until 1968. Bartlett's was a sight to behold, housed in an old tugboat that had been sunk into the ground up to its decks. In the intervening years after it closed, the tug was dug up and removed, and an old army barracks from a nearby base was moved to the property. The existing building was eventually framed and built with wood milled from trees that were felled by a hurricane that had battered the coast. Once the shack was finished, it became a combination clam shack and ice-cream parlor and has remained one ever since.

Owners Keith and Kathy Malinowski bought the building and the business back around 1980 and renamed it the Ice House. Keith was raised in Milwaukee, Wisconsin, and his parents ran a neighborhood tavern there named Ice House Mary's. The name of his New Hampshire clam shack is a tribute of sorts to his parents. It's a charming building: wooden, two stories tall, gabled in a couple of spots in front, and a classic clam shack–style roof overhang above the order windows.

There's a large menu suspended over the windows, where it faces customers standing in line while

**ICE** House owner Keith Malinowski.

mulling over what to order. An indoor dining room with booths of varnished, knotty pine is reminiscent of Malinowski's woodsy Wisconsin and serves as a cozy place to be waited upon for lunch or dinner. Most people order out front and dine in the rough out back at one of the many colorful picnic tables that look out on a nearby golf course.

Once you ditch your car or bike in the gravel parking lot (it's a great area for cycling, by the way), it's time to get in line, step up onto a long, narrow wooden deck with rails and flower boxes, and place your order. It's a classic clam shack–style experience, except that the Ice House is a tad more dressed up than many other shacks, perhaps due to its upscale neighborhood in Rye and its proximity to tony New Castle, New Hampshire.

## Keeping the Locals Happy

Because the customer base is mostly local, the Malinowskis are personal friends with many of the regular patrons. Keith regularly works the indoor dining room, shaking hands and catching up on (or dispensing) the latest local news. He and Kathy have recently taken more of a back seat in the business, while their daughter Meghan and son-in-law Drew have stepped up and are now running many of the day-to-day operations.

And there's plenty to keep them busy. Keith says the Ice House cuts, breads, and fries fifty pounds of onion rings per day in the summer, and in one recent summer season, they served over fifty thousand gallons of ice cream. The staff is youthful—"anywhere from high school kids to people with master's degrees," says Keith.

**MANY** states are represented in the Ice House's wood-paneled dining room.

Many have been with the shack for a number of years. Between the kitchen, dining room, ice-cream station, and order windows, it takes more than a dozen energetic workers to keep the place humming on a busy summer day.

## THE FISH 'N' RINGS ARE TOPS

The most popular items on the menu are the fried haddock sandwich and the onion rings. Generous chunks of fresh haddock, sliced tomato, and leafy lettuce are piled onto a sesame seed bun for a sandwich that stands several inches high before you compress it with your hands to make it manageable. The haddock is flaky and tender, and the Ice House's homemade tartar sauce is the perfect complement. The rings are battered and perfectly fried, with the sweetness of the onion sealed in and the battered breading not oily or overcooked. They're a perfect combination for a snack or meal.

Other standouts on the menu include the baked, stuffed haddock or scallops, or a combination of the two. The homemade stuffing on the baked dishes has plenty of shrimp, scallop, and lobster meat in it. You can get a full plate of baked stuffed fish along with a salad and baked potato at a very reasonable price. This is the way to go if you're looking to avoid the deep fryer or the grill. There are also several broiled seafood dishes.

**KEEP** your eyes peeled for this folksy sign when in Rye, New Hampshire.

Chowder comes in a variety of forms that are rotated throughout the week. Depending on the day you're here, you may treat yourself to a wonderfully fresh, homemade bowl of fish, corn, scallop, seafood, or clam chowder.

## BEFORE YOU GO . . .

Ice cream is a big deal here. Be sure to grab a cone or dish or, better yet, try one of the dozen or so custom-made sundaes from the Ice House's busy fountain. Of particular note is the Kitchen Sink: a mega-sundae with ice cream, hot fudge, strawberries, pineapple chunks, bananas, marshmallow, nuts, sprinkles, and whipped cream. Enough said.

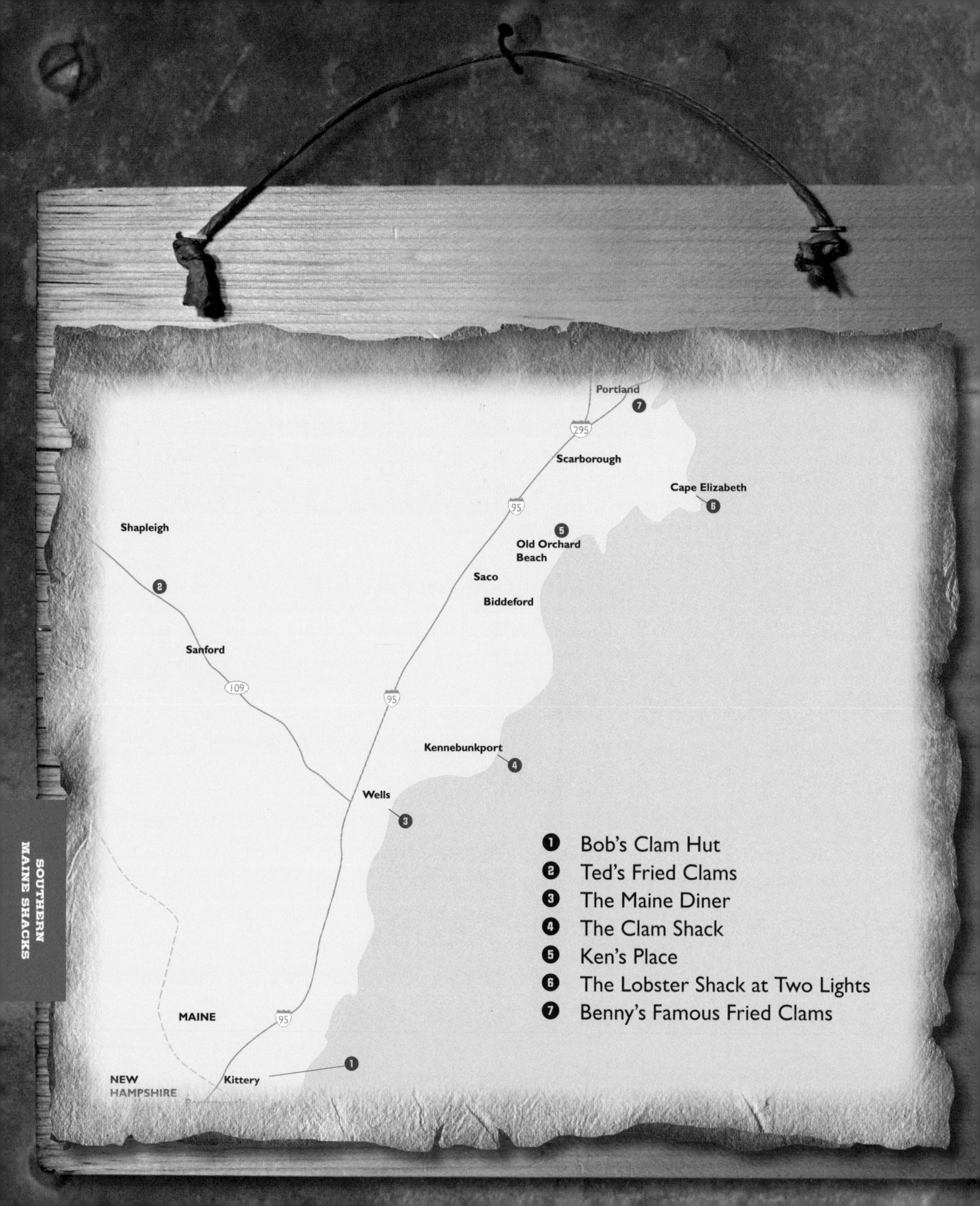

Portland

295

Scarborough

Cape Elizabeth
6

95

5
Old Orchard
Beach

Saco

Biddeford

Shapleigh

2

Sanford

109

95

Kennebunkport
4

Wells

3

1 Bob's Clam Hut

2 Ted's Fried Clams

3 The Maine Diner

4 The Clam Shack

5 Ken's Place

6 The Lobster Shack at Two Lights

7 Benny's Famous Fried Clams

MAINE

95

NEW
HAMPSHIRE

Kittery

1

# SOUTHERN MAINE SHACKS

**W**hen you motor north on I-95 and cross the Piscataqua River Bridge into Kittery, Maine, things start to feel a little different right away. Images of lobsters and pine trees will start popping up on road signs, and thoughts of rocky Atlantic coastlines and picturesque lighthouses may start taking shape in your mind.

Maine is a special place that attracts a certain type of people. It's sort of like the Alaska of the Northeast. Independent-minded individuals feel right at home here, among the wooded landscape, the moose, the loons, and the overall peacefulness and fresh air that on a good day can make you feel reborn.

Although more densely populated than most of the rest of the state, southern Maine still has a distinctly rural feel to it. Drive down any road, and you're sure to come across people selling vegetables from their gardens at roadside stands. Every coastal town, and even many inland ones in southern Maine, have at least several independent-minded citizens who sell live lobsters from cold tanks in their garages or outbuildings or trucks.

Clam shacks here are plentiful and full of character. Each one has a special story to tell and offers many wonderful dishes of local seafood prepared fresh and creatively.

# Bob's Clam Hut

315 Route 1, Kittery, ME 03904 | (207) 439-4233 | www.bobsclamhut.com | Open year-round

The clam shack scene in Maine begins with a bang at Bob's Clam Hut, right off exit 3 of I-95, just a mile or so across the border from New Hampshire in the town of Kittery. Bob's is a huge, bustling shack that in the summer can take on the look and feel of Logan Airport during the holiday season. There can be literally hundreds of people swarming Bob's complex of buildings and outdoor dining areas, yet the well-trained staff can handle just about any size crowd that comes their way.

Bob's has grown greatly over the years while sticking closely to its original formula for success. Situated next to Spruce Creek, the shack is smack-dab in the middle of Kittery's outlet mall zone on Route 1. Bob's growth over the years has more than kept pace with the increasing number of shoppers and tourists who flock to this Maine border town for a little shopping and some good eats.

**BOB'S** sells clams and so much more.

## WHO IS BOB?

The Bob's Clam Hut story starts back in 1956, when Robert Kraft Sr. (not the same Robert Kraft of New England Patriots fame) was living with his family on Route 1 in Kittery, and he got the idea to sell food from the family's yard to passersby on Route 1. (Even then, Kittery was a mecca for tourists, especially from the Boston area, so there was a steady stream of traffic going by.)

Bob enjoyed clamming on the local flats as a kid, and he started shucking and frying up his catch, steadily perfecting his fried clam recipe until he had it just right. Kraft's recipe is still the one used today at Bob's, and the fried clams attract thousands of loyal customers year after year.

Kraft built a modest "hut" in the early days, and the look of the place pretty much remained the same for the next thirty years—a shack with a slightly overhanging roof in the front to provide shade and shelter for the customers lined up at the order and pickup windows.

In 1986, local musician and Bowdoin College graduate Michael Landgarten bought Bob's from Kraft and his wife. While preserving many of the recipes that made the place so popular, Landgarten began adding some dishes of his own. He also started building onto the shack, initially adding an ice-cream wing in 1987.

Within the next three years, the kitchen had been expanded, a shaded eating area created, and then the biggie: a large, enclosed, year-round dining room with a vaulted ceiling and post-and-beam construction.

Since then, lots more outdoor seating has been added, and a pretty white picket fence stretches across the front of Bob's, adding a good measure of psychological (if not actual physical) safety from the almost constant automobile traffic on Route 1.

## Great Food, Friendly Service

So, why do so many people mob this place, especially in the summer? It's simple: the food and the fast, friendly service. First-time customers milling around the order windows often look concerned, thinking they may have to wait for hours for their food to appear. But with ten deep-fryers going full-tilt in high season and a

## Bob's Clam Hut Chowder

Bring a little bit of Bob's fine cooking into your home, even if you're nowhere near the place, with this wonderful recipe for Bob's famous clam chowder. The recipe yields 14 servings.

- 2 medium potatoes, peeled, cut into ¼-inch dice
- 1 small onion, minced
- 1 rib celery, chopped
- 5 cups clam juice, divided
- 1 cup water
- 1 tablespoon fresh thyme (or 1 tablespoon dried)
- 1 tablespoon butter
- 1 tablespoon Worcestershire sauce (or to taste)
- ½ teaspoon salt (or to taste)
  Freshly ground pepper
- 2 cups minced clams
- 4 cups whipping cream

Combine potatoes, onion, celery, 1 cup of the clam juice, water, thyme, butter, Worcestershire, salt, and pepper to taste in a stockpot or Dutch oven. Heat to a boil, stirring often. Reduce the heat; simmer until the potatoes are soft, about 20 minutes.

Stir in the clams, cook for 5 minutes, then add the remaining 4 cups of clam juice and cream to the clam mixture. Heat to a simmer, about 10 minutes. Do not boil.

Enjoy!

**THE** King lives on at Bob's Clam Hut.

lively staff of young and energetic cooks keeping the kitchen humming, most patrons are pleasantly surprised to have their meals in hand before they've had time to take more than a couple sips of their sodas.

The fried clams rule here. They're crispy, sweet, lightly battered, and twice fried in super-clean oil for extra firmness and locked-in flavor. Be sure to load up on the homemade tartar sauce; it's excellent on the clams and the rest of the deep-fried fare. The clams are locally sourced, guaranteeing freshness that many establishments can't really match. Promise, however, that you'll try at least one fried clam unadorned with tartar sauce or lemon; it'll give you a clear picture of what fried clams are supposed to taste like when they're done right.

Another treat from the deep fryer is the haddock, Maine's fish fillet of choice. It's served with various seafood platters and on a very tasty fish sandwich (again, don't forget the homemade tartar sauce). Bob's offers the option of having the fried haddock with the skin on one side— something that gives some diners pause, but try it. It's got a sweet flavor, and it adds some firmness to the fish. Bob's fried haddock, by the way, is so tender and juicy that you'll swear it's been sautéed.

Extraordinary onion rings of the thin, lightly breaded variety are a wise choice for a side order, as is the homemade coleslaw (it comes with the dinners, but be sure to order it on the side if you're going with a seafood roll, a sandwich, or a basket).

Bob Kraft's original clam chowder is another item that put Bob's on the map and keeps it there. Generous chunks of clam and potato are slow-cooked with clam juice, butter, whipping cream, and a variety of spices to make a hearty, flavorful, and filling chowder that's great any time of year. Bob's recently won a chowder competition against forty other restaurants in the Portsmouth, New Hampshire, area, so you know this stuff has to be good!

If clams aren't your thing but you still crave

a warm bowl of something, then try the lobster stew, with many of the same ingredients as the chowder, minus the clams and juice, and fortified with lobster claw, knuckle, and tail meat simmering in a fine, broth-like stew.

## A Bit of Whimsy

As you mill about the expansive grounds, waiting for your meal, keep your eyes out for a couple of Bob's Clam Hut classics. First, there are the murals. Local artist Gordon Carlisle created a life-size rendition of Elvis wearing a Gloucester fisherman's rain slicker and hat, singing into a triple-dip ice-cream cone, and standing confidently atop a large boxed order of fried clams. You'll find this gem next to the order window in the ice-cream annex.

Carlisle also rendered a somewhat schizophrenic mural with several characters from *Gilligan's Island* on the right-hand portion of the piece (playing the part of customers at Bob's) and the left-hand portion showing the hardworking crew in Bob's kitchen. Painted in the middle of this unusual piece between Gilligan and galley crew is a wall calendar with the date May 23, 1986, circled on it. That's the date Michael Landgarten bought the place. And you thought there were lots of hidden clues in Da Vinci's paintings . . .

## Bob's Heart and Soul

The second thing to check out is adjacent to the ice-cream window in the shaded area next to the main shack. It's Lillian's Window, an order window manned by Bob's most senior and adorable employee, Lillian Mangos. There's a sign above the window honoring this matriarch of Kittery clamdom. Lillian has been taking orders from customers at Bob's for a quarter century, and you can see her at the window nearly every day, greeting people, exchanging pleasantries with longtime friends and fans, and sending a lot of orders back into the kitchen behind her, which is staffed mainly by people one-third her age. We should all hold such high places of honor where we work. All hail, Lillian! Be sure to stop by and say hello.

If you're worried about parking at such a busy establishment, take comfort in knowing that during busy stretches, two orange-vested teenagers direct traffic into and out of the parking lot, ensuring a smooth transition between those who are starving and those departing to find a good place to take a nap. Although these sentries may not even be old enough to drive, don't worry—they don't park any cars, they simply wave them in and out of the parking spaces. Be sure to wave good-bye to them and to Bob's as you pull out and start planning your next visit to this little slice of clam heaven.

# Ted's Fried Clams

Route 109, Shapleigh, ME 04076 | **No published phone number** | **www.tedsfriedclams.com**
**Open early March to late October**

**M**ost clam shacks are situated on or near the seashore, close to the sources of all that good seafood. Ted's Fried Clams of rural Shapleigh, Maine, is an exception. A trip to Ted's will take you some twenty miles north of the Maine coast from Wells, through the inland city of Sanford, and up into the state's popular inland lakes region. There are way more pine trees than tidal pools up here, and locals fish for largemouth bass and northern pike, not stripers and bluefish. Yet, when a breeze blows through the stands of pine on a balmy summer day, the soft, whispering sound is reminiscent of the distant Atlantic's gently lapping tidal waters. Welcome to Ted's inland clam empire!

### ⫼ SIXTY YEARS AND COUNTING ⫼

Ted's Fried Clams is no newcomer to the shack scene. It was founded in 1950 by Theodor Mavrakos, a turn-of-the-century Greek immigrant who settled in the Sanford area and who launched a number of small businesses in Sanford before hitting on the idea of a roadside seafood stand. He selected a spot on busy Route 109, the main thoroughfare between Sanford and the lakes to the north, with the idea of pulling in business from the many motorists traveling between city and summer home. He built a modest, whitewashed, one-room shack by the roadside and tacked a sign on the façade that read: TED'S FRIED CLAMS.

Ted passed away in 1953, and his son Harry took over the business. In 1964, Harry replaced the original shack with a three-room building, and he added a bunch of picnic tables outside. An indoor dining room was added in 1976, the

**TED'S** owner, John Mavrakos, making the chowder.

same year Harry's son, John, started working for the family business. John eventually bought out his father and added more indoor dining space on one side and an ice-cream counter on the other side of the now massive structure. The parking lot also grew and now holds over 100 cars. Ted's is a commanding presence on the highway, and it's hard to drive by without being tempted to stop in to see what all the fuss is about.

In a fit of nostalgia, John has preserved Theodor's original shack and moved it to the far end of the main parking lot, where it serves as a sort of museum piece. You should check it out while you're at Ted's. It's a well-known and popular local attraction. Be sure to take note of the prices posted on the hand-painted menu. They're circa early 1960s, when times were simpler (and a heckuva lot cheaper).

## THREE SHACKS IN ONE

There are essentially three businesses running simultaneously at Ted's. First and foremost is the deep-fried seafood, which you may order from the long, gleaming stainless steel counter in the center portion of the building. There are usually up to half a dozen cheerful youngsters ready to take your food and drink order and to hand it over to you when it's ready several minutes later.

### The Greek Connection

Limberakis, Asinakopoulos, Stoilas, Argyriadis, Aggelakis, Mavrakos, Tatakis . . . the list of Greek-owned and -operated clam shacks goes on and on.

What is it about clam shacks that attracts so many Greek-Americans to own and run them? No one knows for sure, except that there is an inclination for Greek immigrants to go into the restaurant business upon arriving in the United States. This is most likely due to the fact that many of their relatives and friends work in the restaurant and food service industries, and it's an easy point of entry into the job market, especially for new arrivals.

Whatever the reason, customers have benefited greatly from so many shacks being Greek-owned and run. Besides all the hard work and attention to detail put into these establishments, who can resist a basket of Greek-style fried calamari or a tasty, refreshing Greek salad chock-full of feta cheese and kalamata olives when it's paired with a heaping deep-fried seafood platter? *Opa!*

Fried whole-belly clams are still the big draw at Ted's. They're somewhat exotic, given the shack's distance from the seashore. Yet a lot of people make huge detours to come here just for a plate of them. John says they fry up

**TED'S** smiling, helpful counter staff.

fifty gallons of shucked clams per week during the busy season. Haddock is also very popular, selling up to 500 pounds per week in the summer. Lots of grilled burgers and hot dogs are sold throughout Ted's full season from March through October. And John has been adding a number of baked seafood dishes to the menu in recent years, with scallops and haddock leading the way.

The second business is Ted's unusual combination chowder bar and lobster bar, both of which are located at the back of the massive indoor dining room. There's a sliding glass window at which you may place an order for a boiled or steamed lobster or for a cup or bowl of Ted's famous clam or haddock chowder or the more substantial lobster stew. The lobster tanks are built into the wall, almost like fish aquariums, and you may pick out your favorite one for your dinner.

Once you've noshed on Ted's tasty and substantial sandwiches, baskets, and dinners, stroll on over to the other side of the building where you'll find Rockhouse Ice Cream, the dessert and sweets portion of the operation. Ted's has been serving ice cream since 2008, and it's become an important part of their business, especially in the twilight hours. There is a dizzying array of some thirty hard-packed ice-cream flavors, including seasonal specials such as blueberry and peach in spring and summer and apple crisp and pumpkin in the fall. The ice cream is available in cups or cones or as part of a single, double, or (gasp) triple sundae with all the toppings. Soft serve is available in vanilla, chocolate, and swirl. Every Thursday is Rockhouse Ice Cream Day, with temptingly discounted prices on ice-cream cones, a particularly strong draw for families on a budget.

Speaking of families, Ted's prides itself on being, above all else, a family-friendly shack, and you can tell from the moment you enter. The dining room is expansive and clean and has

**THE** original Ted's Fried Clams shack, which serves as a museum piece and tourist attraction, sits at one end of the massive parking lot.

the look and feel of a mid-American family restaurant. In addition, there's a separate outdoor dining area with picnic tables right next to the Rockhouse Ice Cream operation. Rockhouse even has its own service window facing the outdoor dining area, in addition to the main service counter inside the building itself.

## No Phone-in Orders

There's one quirk to Ted's that is unusual for a clam shack—or any restaurant, for that matter: There's no listed phone number, so the only way to learn more about Ted's or to make contact with the place is via their website or their Facebook page. John feels strongly that having a phone-in/carryout business is not in his best

interest or in the best interest of his customers. He believes that, once his made-to-order deep-fried seafood is ready, it starts losing its quality from the second it's bagged and handed over to the customer. That's the main reasoning behind his large seating capacity—he wants you to enjoy his food while it's hot and at its best. You may, of course, still come in and order your food to go, but you would do well to follow John's advice, sit down, and enjoy some deep-fried goodies in the woodsy setting of Shapleigh, Maine.

# Nothing Could Be Finah than
# Fried Clams at the Maine Dinah

Any clam shack worth its tartar sauce takes its customers' food orders at a window or counter and calls out order numbers so customers can fetch their food when it's ready. It's the essence of in-the-rough dining. Nearly every establishment in this guide adheres to this cardinal rule in one way or another.

We're going to bend the rules a bit with **The Maine Diner**. This place on Route 9 in Wells, Maine, is so extraordinary, and it does such wonderfully unique and tasty seafood dishes (including deep-fried seafood and lobster rolls) that it deserves special recognition. Plus, it has all the good vibes and warm feelings that shacks share with their customers. So, the Maine Diner is hereby decreed to be an "honorary clam shack."

Although the Maine Diner's menu is laden with all sorts of standard diner fare, such as turkey and chicken platters, beef stew, chili, mac and cheese, and dozens of salads and sandwiches, it's their seafood that puts this place on the culinary map.

### Lobsters and Scallops and Clams, Oh, My!

Most likely because it's in Maine, lobster dominates the seafood offerings in the form of lobster rolls (hot and cold varieties), lobster stew, and Maine Diner's mind-bending lobster pie, made from a secret family recipe.

Don't pass up the deep-fried whole-belly clams, which hail from Nova Scotia. Manager Jim MacNeill claims these Canadian bivalves are smaller and have better flavor than their American counterparts. If you really need to get your clam fix, try the Clam-O-Rama, a medley of clam chowder, fried whole-belly clams and clam strips, and a luscious clam cake. Deep-fried scallops, gulf shrimp, and haddock are also on the menu.

Co-owners Myles and Dick Henry ate here when they were kids, and when the diner came up for sale in 1983, they decided to buy it. They were intent on keeping the diner's spirit alive while importing a bunch of unique recipes from their parents and grandparents, and through lots of hard work, they've succeeded beyond their wildest dreams.

A bona fide clam shack the Maine Diner is not, but it's such a unique and satisfying Maine dining experience that it would be a shame not to include it with all the other wonderful seafood shacks on New England's coastline.

**THE** Maine Diner has some of the best fried seafood in the state.

# The Clam Shack

**2 Western Avenue, Kennebunkport, ME 04046 | (207) 967-3321 | www.theclamshack.net**
**Open early May to mid-October**

o find Kennebunkport's fabled Clam Shack, it's probably better to use your instincts and eyes (or GPS) rather than search for its 2 Western Avenue street address. Just take Route 9 into downtown Kennebunkport, where there's a short bridge spanning the Kennebunk River smack in the center of town. On the Kennebunk (west) side of the river, you'll find the Clam Shack in all its pint-sized glory perched on the edge of the bridge, dangling over the river and almost always crowded with eager diners queued up at the order window and stretching down the street, waiting for some of the best seafood to be had in Maine.

**THE** deceptively modest Clam Shack of Kennebunkport, Maine.

This is as authentic as clam shacks get. No muss, no fuss, lots of whitewashed, understated character, and plenty of good deep-fried seafood, rolls, and chowder. Owner Steve Kingston likes keeping the Clam Shack and its operations simple and unadorned. It's an approach that has worked very well for him (and for many other successful shack owners throughout New England), and it's an approach that Steve has worked to perfection.

From Mother's Day weekend through Columbus Day, the Clam Shack serves tens of thousands of meals to the crowds of tourists who tread the streets of Kennebunkport, searching for gifts, good ice cream, and great food. Its reputation is based on its unwavering attention to quality and consistency, and customers vote their approval with their patronage year after year.

## A Brief Clam Shack History

The little white building by the bridge started as a seafood market in 1938, next to the bustling commercial fishing docks of Kennebunkport. In 1968, a man named Richard Jacques bought the seafood market and added a carry-out shack operation to the mix. Over the next thirty-odd years, Jacques built a strong local brand and a loyal following among locals and the growing crowds of tourists. He focused his offerings on deep-fried clams, clam strips, fish, scallops, and shrimp as well as chowder and lobster rolls—a lineup very similar to today's Clam Shack menu.

In the mid-1980s, Steve Kingston, a Bates College student who had spent numerous summers in the Kennebunkport area, started a lemonade push-cart business in town, having been inspired by a college friend who opened a similar business in Hanover, New Hampshire. Kingston sold some 15,000 fresh-squeezed lemonades that summer, which helped to pay for his college tuition, and it ignited his entrepreneurial spirit. He continued his lemonade business for the next few summers. The Aunt Marie's Ice Cream shop in town came up for sale, and he added it to his burgeoning summer retailing empire.

Steve continued to run these businesses for several years, staffing them with student workers during the summer while he embarked on a sales career with a paper wholesaler. Then, during the Christmas holiday in 1999, he had an epiphany as he drove over the river bridge in Kennebunkport and noticed a FOR SALE sign on Jacques's clam shack building. "I knew then what I wanted to do for the rest of my working life," he says. Steve outbid other interested parties for the shack and seafood market, and he took possession in 2000, his first season as owner/operator of the Clam Shack and seafood market. After a trying first few seasons, he has been the happy owner ever since.

## An Award-Winning Lobster Roll

The Clam Shack's menu has always been, and will most likely always be, a simple lineup of basic seafood fare, deep-fried to perfection with unwavering consistency and quality. The tiny kitchen in back of the shack's order and pickup windows is designed for quick, simple food preparation. By not cluttering the menu with a lot of offerings and keeping the kitchen operation lean and mean, Steve and his crew can concentrate on doing a few things very well.

The Shack's signature dish is its lobster roll. Served either with warm, drizzled butter or cold with a dash of mayo, each roll is heaped with just-cooked lobster meat—not pre-cooked or pre-picked, refrigerated meat. When you order your roll, your lobster is cooked and picked to order, and your sandwich is prepared on the spot. The buns are of the hamburger type, baked fresh daily at Reilly Bakery in nearby Biddeford. They're light and fluffy, and they do a great job

# The Lobster Summit

Kennebunkport's most famous residents are George H. W. Bush and wife Barbara. The Bush family has had a seaside home in the area for many years, and George and Barbara may be seen around town from time to time, having dinner at a restaurant or doing some shopping.

Several years ago, Clam Shack owner Steve Kingston made the acquaintance of the Bushes' family chef, Ariel DeGuzman, and Kingston started supplying DeGuzman's kitchen with live local lobsters and steamers for Bush family functions.

In 2007, during the administration of son George W. Bush, a U.S.-Russian summit was arranged at the Bush family's Kennebunkport estate. In addition to all the weighty issues that the Americans and Russians had to discuss at the meeting, some interesting and unusual events were added to the agenda. Pere Bush took his son and President Putin fishing in his boat off Maine's rocky coast, and he wanted to show Vladimir what it was like to enjoy the fruits of the New England seashore.

One big question (at least on the minds of the European and Russian press) was what would be served to Putin for the state dinner that was to be part of the meeting. Reporters from Europe and Russia were clamoring to find out what was on the menu. DeGuzman decided on a simple New England meal featuring lobster, and Kingston was called upon to provide and prepare the crustaceans in the traditional New England manner.

As soon as word got out that Steve and his Clam Shack were providing the main course, he was deluged with requests for information and interviews from visiting reporters—a Russian television station even interviewed him in front of the Clam Shack, asking him about the strange and unusual American dish he was going to provide for the dinner.

The dinner choice for Putin's visit inspired the media to nickname the high-level meeting the "Lobster Summit." Although the talks didn't accomplish anything substantive, it certainly served as a warm cultural exchange between the Bushes and their Russian guest, and Steve's lobsters were at the center of it.

Since then, Steve has maintained a close relationship with DeGuzman and the Bushes. He frequently prepares clam bakes, grilled swordfish, and other local seafood specialties for Bush family functions. Although you may not see the Bushes lined up outside the Clam Shack's order window any time soon, you can nonetheless be assured that they're big fans of the place.

of containing the sandwich's copious amounts of lobster meat.

In the early 2000s, *USA Today* named the Clam Shack's lobster roll one of the "50 Great Plates" of food in America. There was one Great Plate from each state, and the Clam Shack's roll was the winner in Maine. More recently, the Shack's sandwich was pitted against another lobster roll from Alisson's Restaurant in Kennebunkport on the Travel Channel's *Food Wars* program, and Steve's roll prevailed.

## From the Fryers and Chowder Pot

On the deep-fried side of things, you really can't go wrong. The Clam Shack's namesake whole-belly clams are of local Maine origin; they're very lightly breaded and fried to perfection in super-clean oil. Scallops and shrimp are of equally high quality, served on platters and in generously portioned rolls.

The haddock comes in bite-size chunks, lightly breaded and deep-fried. It comes from faraway Iceland via North Cove Seafood in Boston, which makes daily deliveries of the super-fresh fish directly to the Shack's receiving room.

The clam chowder is another standout. It's from a recipe originally developed by Richard Jacques that Steve has tweaked a bit, primarily by adding more clam meat to each serving. It's got a rich, milky broth (solidly in the Maine tradition), and it's chock-full of perfectly cooked potatoes and at least one ounce of fresh sea clam meat in each serving.

## I've Got My Food, Now What Do I Do?

One thing you'll notice at the Clam Shack is that there's not an abundance of space to sit down and enjoy your repast. Because of the Shack's small amount of real estate on the bridge, you sometimes have to get creative about where to eat. There are several wooden benches with rustic wooden boxes that serve as tables positioned right next to the seafood market, and a few café tables have recently been installed in the market itself. Other than that, you may either have your meal standing up or take it with you back home.

No matter what you select from the Clam Shack's spare menu, you really can't go wrong. It's a testament to Steve and to the Shack that, if you do something that your customers like and you do it well, there's no reason to change things, and your consistency and commitment will keep them coming back for more.

# Ken's Place

207 Pine Point Road, Scarborough, ME 04074 | (207) 883-6611 | Open May through October

Less than a mile from popular Old Orchard Beach in Scarborough, Maine, is Ken's Place, a seafood emporium that dates back longer than most clam shacks in Maine, or coastal New England, for that matter.

Ken Skillings opened his eponymous seafood stand in his garage way back in 1927. He and a few buddies dug sea clams on the local flats, and he started cooking up clam cakes and fried clams and selling them out of the garage. Skillings got lots of business from the locals, and he soon opened an early version of the Ken's Place stand on Pine Point Road in a spot somewhat closer to the beach than its current location.

## DINE BENEATH THE PINES

Ken eventually sold the business to the Bergeron family in 1963, and they kept it going strong for the next thirty-seven years, eventually moving Ken's to its current location in its gray-painted wooden roadhouse building. They added enclosed dining areas on each side of the original building, with windows wrapping around the sides for more sunlight.

These expansions displaced a number of Ken's outdoor picnic tables, which Bergeron relocated to an open field in back of the building. For many years, an additional number of picnic tables have been nestled in a small pine forest toward the back of the shack's five-acre property. Generations of customers fondly recall dining with their families in the pine grove; the tables remain, and the tradition continues today.

As the Bergerons tired of the business in the late 1900s, along came Dave Wilcox, a thin,

**DAVE** Wilcox, the energetic owner of Ken's Place.

energetic food service manager who had been running the Lobster Cooker Restaurant in Freeport, Maine, for eighteen years. Dave bought Ken's, and he took off like a rocket, cleaning up and remodeling the aging shack. In the ten years that he has owned it, Dave has quadrupled the amount of business.

Ken's has a decidedly family feel to it, with lots of picnic tables and indoor booths for six or more diners. Dave and his wife have three kids; perhaps that's what inspired the family-size seating arrangements. Plus, the big field, which is still in back, is the perfect place to exile your restless herd, should they tire of sitting with mom and dad for any length of time during lunch or dinner.

## Fresh Seafood's the Key

Wilcox believes that a lot of his success is attributable to the freshness of the seafood that he serves at Ken's Place. He has thirty years of experience procuring seafood in the Portland area, and he knows where to go for the freshest, best wholesale seafood around. Virtually all his product is sourced locally. He buys from local clam diggers, scallop boats, lobstermen,

**FOUNDER** Ken Skilling, his son, and wait staff, circa 1946.

and haddock fishermen. There is one person in Dave's kitchen who is an experienced and dedicated fish cutter; he fillets up to 100 fresh haddock daily for the restaurant. And at the raw bar, situated in a corner of the dining room, a regularly featured item is the Belon oysters, which have been transplanted from France and are now harvested from oyster beds in the nearby Nonesuch River.

With all this great seafood at Ken's to choose from, where should one begin? Actually, it's not hard—start with the battered fried clams. Ken's is one of the few establishments in Maine that offers its fried clams coated in your choice of batter or crumbs; the batter version is a happy revelation for those who haven't tried it. Light and crunchy, these smooth-surfaced, golden brown clam nuggets seal in the sweetness and salinity perfectly and offer a wonderful alternative to the somewhat weightier whole bellies drenched in the crumb mix.

## CLAM CAKES ON MOTHER'S DAY

Clam cakes are still a popular item on the menu. They sell like crazy on Mother's Day, which is the busiest day of the year at Ken's, when they serve some 2,000 customers. The cakes are firm and full of flavorful minced clam and lightly seasoned for a bit of a kick.

Lobster rolls are another big seller. Dave does his in a light mayo mixture served cold on a split-top bun. Hot buttered lobster is also available for those who prefer theirs warm. Ken's has a couple of kitchen workers picking fresh lobster meat all day every day; 200 picked lobsters per day is the norm—a tedious task that yields great rewards.

Whether fried or baked, the haddock must be singled out, also. This fish is everything Wilcox boasts about and more. It's incredibly light and flaky and has that fresh and mild flavor of the sea that all properly prepared fish ought to have. Fillets are substantial, so bring an appetite and be prepared to take some home.

## HOME-GROWN SHRIMP

Ever tried deep-fried Maine shrimp? These guys are small, sweet, and delectably chewy, and they're even better when they're enjoyed with cocktail or tartar sauce. The shrimp are harvested in the Gulf of Maine during the winter months, then they're frozen and served up throughout the summer.

The chowders and lobster stew don't disappoint, and they make a fine complement to a plate of clam cakes. The clam chowder is of the New England variety with the Maine twist—that is, it's not really thick like the kind you get in the Boston area. It's made with less cream and more milk for a more fluid consistency. It's a

**LOBSTER** picking is a constant activity in Ken's busy kitchen.

nice, spicy chowder made with red potatoes, as is the wonderful fish chowder. Both come in cup and bowl sizes. The lobster stew is more substantial in quantity but also on the lighter side in terms of the broth. But it's packed with flavor and lots of that picked-daily-on-the-premises lobster meat.

Baked seafood dishes are on the rise at Ken's, both in variety and popularity. The two biggies are the baked haddock and baked sea scallops. The seafood is lightly breaded, placed on an ovenproof, oval-shaped paper plate, and put into the oven. The haddock and scallops are, if anything, even fresher tasting when prepared this way, and it's certainly a healthy alternative to the ever-popular deep-fried dishes. You may also get a combo plate—half deep-fried, half

baked—in case you're straddling the fence and not sure which way to go.

## GOODIES FROM THE GRILL

John is justifiably proud of the burgers at Ken's. They're made with 90 percent lean, pure Angus beef, and they're very popular with the locals and the non-seafood crowd. The hot dogs are all beef, and the grilled cheese sandwich clocks in at under $3, a good choice for any seafood-fearing youngsters.

You may make a meal of the grilled chicken salad or perhaps opt for a salad plate, which comes in egg, tuna, crabmeat, and lobster varieties. Each plate includes an avalanche of fresh veggies, sliced hard-boiled eggs, grated cheese, pickles, and even a dollop of potato salad. Diet plates these are not!

The raw bar is a welcome addition that debuted way back in 1987. Fresh local oysters and clams are the main draw, along with beer, wine, and cocktails. Lots of beachgoers and boaters end up here after a hot day in the sun.

Years of hard work and listening to his customers have paid off for John. He has made Ken's a place that you really shouldn't pass up if you happen to be visiting Old Orchard Beach and you're in the mood for some super-fresh seafood and perhaps a quiet moment or two under the whispering pines.

# The Lobster Shack at Two Lights

**225 Two Lights Road, Cape Elizabeth, ME 04107 | (207) 799-1677 | www.lobstershacktwolights.com**
**Open late March to late October**

Cape Elizabeth, just south of Portland, is a dreamy, rural-like setting of farm houses, rolling hills, leafy trees, and the occasional plowed field. The town has worked hard over the years to keep it that way, and the fact that it's on the ocean makes it that much nicer.

GPS is your best guide when searching for the Lobster Shack at Two Lights, as it can be a bit tough to find. You drive down twisting, tree-shaded residential streets for several miles, following signs to Two Lights State Park. As you draw close to the park entrance, you need to veer to the left and continue down the road as it heads toward the coast. Just when you begin to think you've made a wrong turn into a quaint neighborhood of pretty little beach houses, bingo!—you find yourself dead-ending into the parking lot of the Lobster Shack at Two Lights.

**CAPE** Elizabeth Light.

After ascending a short series of steps from the parking lot to the shack, you may temporarily forget about the fine seafood you came in search of and lose yourself in the wondrous view that stretches before you. The Lobster Shack at Two Lights is blessed with a fine perch on the ocean's edge with a cascading wall of rocks separating diners at picnic tables from the crashing surf below. This sun-soaked patio by the sea may be the most distinctive thing about Two Lights, but the food is a close second, and there's plenty to choose from in addition to the namesake lobster.

## GRANDFATHERED INTO THE NEIGHBORHOOD

This happy little shack by the sea got its start way back in the 1920s as a place called the Lobster Shop, where lobster rolls were the house specialty. Baker Jim Ledbetter and his wife, Ruth, bought the place in 1968 and renamed it the Lobster Shack. ("Two Lights" was added later to make the name more distinctive.)

Jim and Ruth set about spiffing the place up,

and they expanded the menu to include deep-fried and grilled items and a broad array of desserts. Some ten years later, their daughter Martha and her husband Herb Porch took over and ran the place until 2005 when their son Jeff and his wife, Katie, became the current owners. Like many great shacks, this is a family-run operation through and through, with cousins and in-laws and (so far) one of Jeff and Katie's five kids all pitching in to help out.

**DINING** right next to the ocean is a big draw at Two Lights.

In some ways, Two Lights is lucky to still be where it is. Had it not been a restaurant for so many years (and hence grandfathered into its location), there is no way anyone could get permission to open a shack business in such a quiet, affluent seaside residential location. As it is, the town only allows Two Lights to be open thirty weeks per year from late March to late October, and their hours of operation are strictly limited to 11 a.m. to 8 p.m. (8:30 in July and August). But it's a very busy thirty weeks, with Two Lights

serving up to 1,500 meals per day in July and August, and the Porches don't seem to mind when they have to close down for the season.

The shack itself is a modest, house-type building with a mostly glass-enclosed back facing the ocean and a short ramp leading into the order area within. Long lines are common in summer, but they move quickly. The Porches have lots of practice handling crowds of hungry visitors.

Once you're inside, you stand face to face with the friendly Two Lights staff behind a long counter with a tempting glass-fronted dessert case in the middle. Place your order, settle your bill, get your number, and head back outside for more of that beautiful view. It won't be long before they call your number over the PA system, and you can either nosh by the seaside or in the small indoor dining area, filled with antique bric-a-brac hanging from the ceiling and walls. (If the weather's nice, there's no reason in the world not to grab a picnic table outside. The view of Casco Bay and the ships entering and leaving Portland harbor is priceless.)

The two lighthouses from which the shack and nearby state park take their names sit about a quarter mile away at two different hilltop spots. Neither is still active, but they make a nice backdrop to the entire scene. There is, however, an active foghorn right next to the Two Lights patio, and it will emit intermittent horn-like bleeps every fifteen seconds or so when conditions warrant. It's a bit startling at first, but it certainly lends a maritime vibe to the whole scene.

## THE LOBSTER ROLL TOPS THE LIST

Make no mistake, the lobster roll is king here. The *Portland Press-Herald* has bestowed its "Best Lobster Roll in the Portland Area" award on Two Lights' sandwich numerous times, and there are plaques suspended above the order counter and on the walls inside to prove it. The recipe is simple: fresh-picked lobster meat served on a New England–style split-top bun with a little bit of lettuce, a crisp pickle slice on the side, and a dollop of mayo on the top, which you may spread around or shoo away, depending on your preference. Martha Porch says they'll make your lobster roll any way you wish, but most people take it in the classic Two Lights style.

In addition to the lobster rolls, lots of people opt for the whole boiled or steamed lobster dinner. Along with your tasty crustacean, you get generous sides of french fries and coleslaw and half a cup of melted butter. About 150 lobster dinners are sold each day at Two Lights in the summer.

The deep fryers at Two Lights are very busy, cooking up large quantities of whole-belly clams, scallops, haddock, and shrimp, which may be had as a "plate" (a big portion of seafood, with fries, coleslaw, and a homemade biscuit) or as a more modest "boat" (fries and slaw only, with a somewhat smaller quantity of your main course). For the truly famished, there's the belt-busting Fisherman's Plate, with a little bit (actually, a lot) of everything on it.

Clam cakes are also popular. They're lighter than most of the ones you'll find elsewhere, with a crispy crunch when you bit into them. The onion rings are hand-cut and make for a sizeable side dish, especially when ordered with all the other deep-fried goodies.

Two Lights procures its seafood from a variety of sources, all of them local. The Porches pick up their lobsters each morning at New Meadows Lobster in Portland. They sell so much lobster each day that they supplement their own lobster picking with fresh-picked lobster from Klenda Seafood in South Portland. Merrill's Seafood, also in Portland, supplies much of the rest of

Two Lights' seafood needs. Clams come from a variety of sources, all of them local; they go through about sixty gallons of clams per week. A high-volume business, indeed!

If seafood isn't your thing, the grill features an array of surprisingly tasty and affordable burgers and hot dogs. There's a grilled veggie burger for the no-meat/no-fish crowd. New England–style clam chowder and a more substantial lobster stew round out the offerings.

**TWO** Lights' cozy dining room.

Founder Jim Ledbetter's legacy as a baker lives on at Two Lights, where fresh-baked goods come out of the oven every day. Among the most popular desserts are the blueberry mini pies, the whoopie pies, and Two Lights' custom version of Grape Nut pudding.

There are two other fun things to do after you've enjoyed your meal on Two Lights' patio. First, take a stroll around the grounds, especially over to the far side of the foghorn building, where there are a couple of well-worn paths that lead out onto the rocks to the north of the shack. It's a nice place to sit in the sun and get a closer look at the ocean below. (Be careful!) And there's a lovely gift shop on the other side of the shack that's chock-full of Maine and lobster memorabilia, as well as Two Lights shirts, mugs, and hats.

If you have any time or energy left, make a stop by Two Lights State Park on your way back to civilization. Although the lighthouses are not on park grounds, there are more lovely views of the sea and short trails along the rocky shore. It also provides an opportunity to walk off that wonderful meal you just had down the road!

# Benny's Famous Fried Clams

199 West Commercial Street, Portland, ME 04102 | (207) 774-2084 | Open May through November

This out-of-the-way, super funky, urban-industrial clam shack is a definite find for those deep-fried seafood lovers of a more citified and adventurous nature. Situated on a busy road in a commercial zone a mile or so west of downtown Portland and right across the street from some freight tracks and Casco Bay's busy shipping channel, Benny's is a bit of a challenge to locate yet a sweet reward for those curious enough to navigate the industrial neighborhood to find it.

Benny Sawyer, a jack-of-several-trades, founded his eponymous clam shack in 1992. He worked in the auto parts business for twenty years, then in home remodeling for twenty more. As a hobby, he enjoyed frying clams, and throughout his auto parts and remodeling careers, he ran a side business on weekends, cooking clams and selling them at local and regional fairs, including the famous Fryeburg Fair, held every fall in western Maine. He built a ten-foot-by-ten-foot wooden clam shack that he hauled to the fairgrounds, along with a couple of deep fryers and other essential shack gear, and he served up his fried goodies to hundreds of hungry fairgoers at each stop.

## A Flower in the Desert

One day in the early 1990s, while driving through Portland's gritty west-end industrial district, he noticed an old truck stop filling station where the fuel tanks were being dug out of the ground—a sure sign that the business was closing. Seeing the low-slung, shingled truck stop building gave Benny an idea to convert it into a clam shack. The land was owned by a local railroad company, and Sawyer worked out a lease deal with the railroad that continues to

**BENNY'S** ramshackle house of fun in Portland, Maine.

this day. There are some old, abandoned tracks running through the woods in back of Benny's, one of the many reminders of the property's industrial roots and surroundings.

In the intervening years, Benny has added on to the original building in delightfully interesting and unusual ways. There's an elevated deck off the front end with several tables and colorful umbrellas; two have Hawaiian grass-skirt-type trims on them. Adjacent to and in back of the shack, there's another outdoor seating area with half a dozen molded plastic tables and benches under a very utilitarian tarp-like tent. Lobster buoys and various whimsical props add to the kitschy, slap-dash look of these dining spots. Sawyer just keeps adding stuff as it comes along. (There is no indoor seating, by the way.)

As you approach the order window just off the deck, you pass under a translucent green corrugated plastic roof, which envelops you in a warm, greenish glow. Pause here to study the menu on the wall in front of you before ordering. Wherever you look in this greenish alcove, there is plenty more in the way of whimsical decorations to behold. Benny is the principal decorator, and he takes the credit (or blame) for the overall look and feel of the place.

The shack's total lack of pretension and super casual setting may not appeal to everyone, but if you enjoy a relaxed, informal, backyard-type

**A** plate of Benny's famous fried haddock.

atmosphere, you're going to feel right at home here. Benny's fits nicely into the Portland scene, which has a large creative community. The downtown area has plenty of off-the-wall restaurants, bars, and coffee shops. So, Benny's is in good company here and is in fact the deep-fried seafood shack of choice for Portland's café society.

## GOOD, HONEST CLAM SHACK FARE

The food at Benny's is as homemade as the shack's decor. Nothing pre-packaged or conventional here. Just good old-fashioned, down-home, deep-fried fresh seafood. Start with a good-sized cup of chowder (fish or clam) and a couple of homemade clam cakes, fried up fresh from dollops of dough dropped into Benny's deep fryers. Lobster stew and shrimp stew are also available. Chowders and stews rotate on a daily basis and aren't all available every day.

Also for starters, consider ordering the french fries or onion rings. Both are outstanding here: hand-cut from fresh potatoes and onions, perfectly fried, and generously salted. They're among the best items on the menu, and they don't come as side dishes with the seafood dinners.

Fried clams top the deep-fried seafood offerings here, and they may be ordered in a variety of ways: by the pint or quart, as part of a seafood combo dinner (with coleslaw and garlic toast), or in a smaller basket, which comes with fries. The whole-belly clams are battered, not breaded, which makes them all the more unusual and tasty.

Running a close second to the clams is Benny's fried haddock. The fillets are first broken into bite-size chunks, then breaded and deep-fried to a golden brown. This sweet-tasting, flaky, white fish is also excellent in sandwich form, with or without fries on the side.

Maine shrimp are a local delicacy, harvested only in winter, then frozen and fried up during the busy summer months. These North Atlantic shrimp are small and sweet and go well with Benny's homemade tartar sauce. They are also sold by the pint and as a dinner or basket. Benny

recently opened a lobster pound on the other side of the building, serving up fresh boiled lobster for picnic table dining in front of the pound or to take home for feasting. If you prefer your lobster in a roll, Benny's serves a cold one from the order window back on the restaurant side.

For those not into seafood, there is a variety of hamburgers and cheeseburgers in the usual configurations as well as hot dogs and cheese dogs from the grill. Sodas, lemonade, and iced tea are the only beverages served here.

## Sittin' by the Dock of the Jetport

To add to the commercial feel of the place, Benny's sits right under one of the flight patterns for nearby Portland International Jetport, the city's main airport. A steady stream of mid-size jets takes off and lands throughout the day, and it's actually quite nice to lean your head back and make out the tail markings on each passing plane as it soars overhead.

There's a different type of serenity at Benny's, one not often found at other clam shacks up and down the New England coast. It's the peace of mind that you get from stepping back for a little while and watching the steady flow of commerce all around you while you enjoy a platter of seafood expertly prepared by a veteran, itinerant clam-frying devotee of the first order.

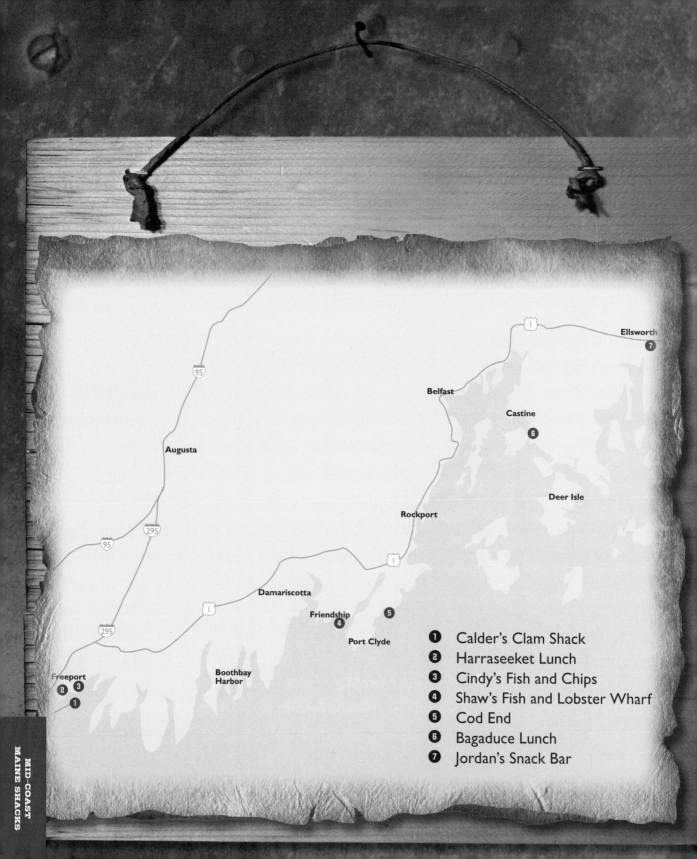

① Calder's Clam Shack
② Harraseeket Lunch
③ Cindy's Fish and Chips
④ Shaw's Fish and Lobster Wharf
⑤ Cod End
⑥ Bagaduce Lunch
⑦ Jordan's Snack Bar

# MID-COAST MAINE SHACKS

**A**lthough you're firmly in lobster country in this scenic, craggy part of Maine, the deep-fried clam still holds its own here very nicely. You'll drive greater distances between clam shacks, but most are so unique and compelling that they're well worth the extra time and effort it takes to reach them.

The deeper you go into mid-coast Maine, the more pronounced the charming Maine accent becomes among locals. From "Freepawt" to "Bah Habah," you're going to meet lots of friendly, plain-spoken people and enjoy some of the finest seafood in all of New England.

A lot of your travels in mid-coast Maine will take you along Route 1, then onto two-lane side roads that head down fingers of land to the sea. Take your time on these meandering drives. Life here goes at a slower pace, and there are lots of great things to see and do in the small towns and fishing villages along the way.

From a front-yard clam shack to a collection of roadside trailer-shacks to a "reversing falls" to a combination country music/deep-fried seafood "theme park," the clam shacks of Maine's mid-coast are as entertaining as they are pleasing to the palate.

# Calder's Clam Shack

**108 North Road, Chebeague Island, ME 04017 | (207) 846-5046 | www.caldersclamshack.com**

**H**ave you ever thought about setting up a clam shack in your front yard? That's exactly what the Calder family has done, with their petite eatery on Chebeague Island, and if you happen to make the journey to this woodsy isle about ten miles distant from Portland and a short ferry ride from the town of Yarmouth, you're in for a unique experience.

Day trippers come to Chebeague to bike and to hike; overnighters stay at the inn on the island and in summer homes that have been passed down through generations of families. There are miles of rocky beaches and even some sandy ones for swimming when tide and temperatures allow. The bulk of the island is heavily wooded, giving the illusion at times that you're nowhere near the ocean. For the past half dozen years and counting, Calder's Clam Shack has been offering what is considered the only truly casual dining experience on the remote and exclusive island.

## VIRGINIA'S PLAYHOUSE

Virginia Tatakis-Calder grew up working in restaurants in central Maine, and after she and her husband, Tom, brought their three children into the world, Virginia yearned to return to the restaurant trade—and bring her family into the business with her. She and Tom drew up plans to build a modest shack by the road in front of their house, approximately a mile from the town dock where the ferry shuttles people back and forth between the mainland and the island.

It's a bit of a surprise when you're on bike or on foot, exploring the wooded, rural island and suddenly you come across a small, whitewashed clam shack by the roadside with an order window, a wall menu, and a galvanized metal

**VIRGINIA** and Tom Calder and their eponymous clam shack.

chimney poking jauntily out of its roof. The sign in front reads CALDER'S CLAM SHACK, but it might just as well read VIRGINIA'S PLAYHOUSE.

Dining at Calder's is a family experience, meaning chances are you'll meet and interact with most, if not all, of the Calder family while you're there. Virginia and Tom do most of the cooking at Calder's. Teenage daughter Tracy helps out in the kitchen, and son Tim and youngest daughter Tiffany linger around the grounds, bussing the picnic tables scattered around the yard.

## LOTS TO CHOOSE FROM

For such a small establishment, Calder's has an amazingly broad and varied menu. Although it's a clam shack by name, deep-fried seafood comprises but a fraction of the offerings. Virginia's Greek-American heritage has left a permanent stamp on the place, as evidenced by the number of dishes with a Hellenic influence.

Perhaps the most popular item at Calder's (with the locals, anyway) is the homemade pizza. Virginia and Tom make their dough from scratch, and there is a wide variety of toppings and special pizza types to choose from. Try the Greek Pizza (feta cheese, spinach, sliced tomatoes, and Greek olives) or the Chebeaguer (heavy on the meat items), or the Shack Attack (onions, green peppers, mushrooms, hamburger, pepperoni, sausage, bacon, ham, and Greek olives—whew!).

Sandwiches are many and varied and are served both hot and cold. There are also several meal-sized salads; the Greek salad is the best pick of the bunch, with baby spinach and iceberg lettuce, ham, provolone cheese, a variety of sliced vegetables, and crumbled feta cheese, tossed with the house Greek dressing. The Calders are increasingly buying their produce from local sources, both for the freshness and to support the few local growers who live on the island.

A shack isn't a shack without fried seafood, and Calder's doesn't disappoint. Virginia and Tom have a straightforward method of preparation, starting with a basic egg-and-milk wash followed by a drenching in cornmeal and flour. You may have any of a number of seafood combinations that include whole-belly clams (no clam strips here), haddock, Maine shrimp, and scallops, all prepared to order. Your best bet is the Stone Slooper, a heaping basket of clams, shrimp, scallops, and haddock accompanied by french fries, homemade coleslaw, and tartar or cocktail sauce.

Calder's clams come from nearby Harpswell via their seafood supplier in Portland. The Maine shrimp at the shack are particularly sweet and tasty, and the haddock comes out of the deep fryer firm, moist, and flavorful. Unlike at most other clam shacks up and down the New England coast, there's no lobster on the menu (particularly surprising for a Maine shack).

## A Town Square Atmosphere

The evening hours bring many locals to Calder's for the Gifford's ice cream, which is served in generous scoops on cones or in strawberry or hot fudge sundaes. The picnic table area at times seems to serve as the unofficial town square, as everyone grabs a spot and swaps stories with tourists and locals alike. Kids can play on the swing set in the Calder's yard, or they can clamber over an old fire truck abandoned in the weeds next to the family barn, where soda and other dry goods are stored. (Tom, a Chebeague Island native, used to be the island's fire chief, and he still serves on the volunteer force.)

To reach the island, you may take a ferry from Portland or from closer-by Cousins Island in Cumberland, where you park in a remote lot, take a shuttle bus to the ferry, and enjoy a delightful fifteen-minute ride across Casco Bay to Chebeague. It's a lot of work for a fried-clam dinner, but if you're up for an interesting day trip to a quiet, friendly coastal island not too far from the mainland, come on over to Chebeague and be sure to stop in and spend some time with the Calders at their front-yard clam shack playhouse.

# Harraseeket Lunch

36 Main Street, South Freeport, ME 04078 | (207) 865-4888 | www.harraseeketlunchandlobster.com
Open early May to mid-October

Harraseeket Lunch is one of the prettiest and most dignified of all the clam shacks to be found in New England. Its blue-and-white canopied dining area in front of the building and its wrought-iron-railed walkway to the lobster pound along the side facing beautiful South Freeport harbor create an atmosphere of casual splendor. Harraseeket's is worthy of a visit for virtually any special occasion, including an outing on Mother's Day or perhaps even a wedding rehearsal dinner in their small, enclosed dining room (check first to make sure it's available).

## In the Beginning, There Was Lobster

Harraseeket's (pronounced Harrah-SEE-kits) got its start in 1971 when founder and current owner Regis Coffin and her then-husband John opened a lobster pound to sell the catch that John pulled daily from his traps offshore. In the beginning, you had the option of taking the lobsters home alive with you or having them cooked up on the spot and enjoying them on nearby picnic tables.

It wasn't long before Regis and John expanded Harraseeket's into a full-fledged shack, serving deep-fried fare and generously portioned seafood rolls. Longtime employee Lucinda Kennedy, who has been with Harraseeket's almost since the beginning, recalls playing cards with her fellow teenage counter workers on the picnic tables out front when things were slow, then jumping to attention and competing for customers (and their tips) when things picked up during busy times of the day.

Lucinda will tell you that there's no longer any time for card playing, as Harraseeket's is buzzing from the moment it opens the restaurant at 11 a.m. until it closes in the early evening. (The

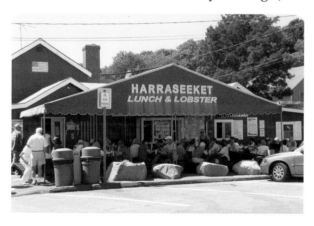

**HARRASEEKET'S** packs 'em in throughout the summer.

## The Ipswich Shellfish Company

Back in 1935, George Pappas and Joe Sikora of Ipswich, Massachusetts, decided to launch a fresh seafood business with the help of several local clam diggers, and the Ipswich Shellfish Company came into being during the depths of the Great Depression.

Within several years, Pappas and Sikora had seventy clam diggers working the nearby beds and seventy-five clam shuckers working in the company's Ipswich headquarters. Sikora sold his share of the business to Pappas, who had a dream of becoming a major seafood supplier in the metro Boston area. His customer base continued to grow as he supplied fresh clams, lobsters, and scallops to a wide variety of wholesale clients, including many of the first clam shacks.

Over the years, Ipswich Shellfish has become a national distribution operation with major facilities in Ipswich, two in Maine, one in Connecticut, and one each in Maryland and South Carolina. All told, the company sells more than 300 million pounds of shellfish annually.

If you're at a clam shack that boasts serving Ipswich clams, you know that you're in for some quality product. When it comes to clams, Ipswich is about as good as it gets in New England—and anywhere else for that matter.

lobster pound opens a little earlier, at 7:00 a.m.) Like at any really good clam shack, wait time to place your order can sometimes be lengthy, so you may wish to time your visit to avoid the peak lunch and dinner hours if you'd like a little more peace and quiet and a quicker turnaround on your order.

### SEAFOOD HOT, COLD, AND STEAMED

There are a couple of food order windows under the blue-and-white-striped canopy on the front side of the building and a large menu nailed to the wall so you can weigh your options while you wait in line. Harraseeket's fresh fish sandwich is one of the most popular items, along with the tasty cold lobster roll, served with or without mayo (your choice). Fried clams are lightly breaded and fried to a crispy crunch; have them as part of a dinner plate, as a side order (half- and full-pint sizes), or on a split-top, toasted, buttered New England–style bun.

If you want to treat yourself to a boiled lobster, steamed clams, crabs, red potatoes, or steamed corn, just walk around the side of the building that faces the harbor (gorgeous view!) and step up to the order window for the lobster pound, which occupies the back half of the building. The South Freeport harbor is still a working harbor, and lobsters are off-loaded from the boats straight into Harraseeket's cold-water tanks inside. Talk about freshness!

## PIES, WHOOPIE AND OTHERWISE

Another hallmark of dining at Harraseeket's is its fine and extensive dessert menu. There's a separate window for dessert and ice-cream orders in front—that's how much emphasis is put on the sweet side of things. Pies top the list, and they come in a variety of home-baked choices: blueberry, apple, strawberry rhubarb, lemon meringue, chocolate cream, and more.

Perhaps the best-known and most popular dessert offering is Harraseeket's own home-made whoopie pies—two mounds of chocolate cake with cream frosting sandwiched between. People come from far and wide to enjoy these sweet and fluffy delicacies, and sometimes it's the only thing they'll order. Lucinda recalls a customer who recently had Harraseeket's ship him two of their whoopie pies so he could present them to his girlfriend when he proposed. (How could she say no?!)

## YOUNG 'UNS WELCOME

Harraseeket's frequently plays host to busloads of campers and scouts from all over New England who are passing through Freeport on their way to or from camp. Lucinda says that often there are kids in these groups who have never seen a lobster and who must be adventurous and take that leap of faith when it comes to noshing on fresh boiled and deep-fried seafood for the first time. Harraseeket's is more than accommodating to these first-timers, giving them tours of the lobster pound and the dock area and providing an unforgettable experience for children who are often raised far from the sea.

A couple of things to keep in mind before high-tailing it down to Harraseeket's. First, it can be tough to find. You'll be convinced that you're not going the right way as you drive down street after leafy street of cute, comfortable homes with nary a road sign indicating that the shack lies anywhere nearby. GPS should guarantee your safe and expeditious arrival, but if you prefer printed maps to help you get around, don't hesitate to slow down and ask the locals if you think you may be lost. They'll let you know how you're doing.

Second, Harraseeket's doesn't accept credit cards. Like many popular shacks, it's cash only. There is an ATM on the premises that accepts major bank and credit cards, so don't be deterred by the "No Plastic" proclamation; you can still enjoy some of the finest food in one of the most scenic locations in all of southern Maine—and don't forget that whoopie pie to go!

# Cindy's Fish & Chips

292 U.S. Route 1, Freeport, ME 04032 | (207) 865-1635 | Open mid-May to mid-September

**W**hen you head south out of Freeport, Maine, on Route 1, a few miles down the road you'll come across Cindy's Fish & Chips, a colorful, dilapidated collection of trailers on the west side of the road, wedged between busy U.S. 1 and the even busier I-295 in back. It looks like a bunch of gypsies set up camp on the roadside, hung out an "Open for Business" sign, and started frying up some clams. The weather-beaten look of Cindy's may give some travelers pause, but if you decide to take a pass on stopping and checking this place out, it's going to be your loss.

**CINDY'S** shaded dining area, with superfluous air-conditioner.

## A CIRCUS ATMOSPHERE

Fans of the HBO series *Carnivale* will feel right at home here. There's a certain wind-blown feel to the place, as if the owners might pick up any minute and hit the road for greener pastures. Cindy's consists of a few well-worn trailers—one that serves as the main shack for cooking and serving up food and the other two that house auxiliary kitchen appliances and supplies. There's also a *ton* of playful kitsch scattered around the premises—everything from stuffed animals and dolls to a Frankenstein statue to a singing, dancing toy lobster that makes even the most sourpussed kid light up with laughter.

If, after surveying the grounds, you're wary of what the food may be like at Cindy's, consider this: No less an authority than Michael N. Marcus, founder and creator of the website www.weloveclams.com, declared that Cindy's makes "The Best Fried Clams on Earth." This is quite an endorsement, given that Marcus truly knows plenty about fried clams, having traveled up and down the Eastern Seaboard many times in search of the best ones and chronicling his findings on his website.

## The Captain of the Ship

Cindy's cantankerous owner, Bob Pottle, is a restless soul who founded this unusual eatery and named it after his daughter in 1980. Nearly always dressed in a clean, white T-shirt, work pants, and well-worn white sneakers, Bob is an ever-present fixture at Cindy's who is usually found tending the deep fryers in the stand's galley-like kitchen behind the order window. Although his back is to the customers while he's cooking, he hears everything they say, and it's rare when he doesn't turn and strike up a conversation or add a comment to an ongoing discussion.

The septuagenarian Pottle got started in the culinary field right out of school in 1947 when he landed a baking job at a hotel in Brunswick, Maine. He spent the next ten or so years baking for various hotels before changing careers and going into the oil burner business. Cindy's Fish & Chips has benefited from Bob's early years as a baker, as he makes some of the finest pies in the Freeport area. You'll find them daily on the shack's dessert menu.

**BOB** Pottle, Cindy's founder and owner.

> ### Closed on Saturdays? What's Up with That?
>
> Bob and Freeda Pottle are Seventh-Day Adventists, which means they don't work on Saturdays. This may seem like lunacy in the tourist- and weekend-dependent clam shack business, but the Pottles adhere strictly to the practices of their beliefs. So, don't plan on visiting Cindy's on a Saturday because it won't be open.

Cindy's is a family-run operation, with Bob's wife Freeda a constant presence at the stand, along with two of their granddaughters. (The namesake daughter Cindy never really got involved in the business.) Freeda is the perfect foil to Bob's constant opinionating. With her poker-faced, sardonic responses to his more outrageous declarations, Freeda plays the part of *The Honeymooner's* long-suffering Alice to Bob's thoroughly Ralph Cramden–type personality.

## What Makes Cindy's Clams So Great

Cindy's opened its doors in 1980, when Bob found a nice little piece of land on Route 1 where he could get back into the food business by having his own place on his own terms. After the first two weeks, customers were already coming back, won over by the stark originality of Bob's roadside cooking, especially his chowders and fried clams.

The secret to Pottle's delectable clams seems to be the batter in which he cooks them. Bob is one of a minority of clam shack chefs who dips his clams in messy batter instead of cornmeal, flour, or bread or cracker crumbs. The end result is a shiny, crispy outer crust that seals in the natural flavor of the clams perfectly. There's a bit of a crunch when you bite in, then the sweet clam-belly flavor takes hold, and you're hooked.

He uses the same approach with his other fried goodies, perhaps to greatest success with his hand-cut onion rings. These delicacies are very sweet (could it be Vidalia onions? Bob won't say); they're lightly spiced and salted—just enough to bring out the pure essence of flavor from the onion within. Bob's oil of choice is soy, and he gets it really hot so that it seals in the flavors of his deep-fried foods quickly. French fries are hand-cut daily from sacks of potatoes stored in one of the auxiliary trailers, and they're cooked in their own deep fryer so as not to mix flavors with the clams and other seafood.

Bob also likes to brag about his coleslaw and tartar sauce, and with good reason. Both are whipped up each morning in one of the trailers, and they add immensely to the shack's reputation for originality. The lobster and crab rolls are heaped high with hand-picked meat and lightly mixed with mayo. They're among the most popular items at Cindy's.

The clam chowder, smoky, rich, and imbued with home-cooked flavor, is another strong point here. Generous portions of clam and chunks of diced potato mix in a flavorful broth that's creamy but not artificially thickened. Cindy's lobster stew is made to order, not dredged from a pot cooked up earlier in the day, and each serving contains six ounces of lobster meat sautéed in butter and dry sherry, then blended with milk and cream. A bowl of this piquant stew is definitely a meal in itself.

## DON'T LEAVE WITHOUT DESSERT!

Back to Bob and his baking: Pies are a regular feature on the dessert board, and they vary depending on what fruit is in season or what looks freshest at the local market. There's also an upside-down cake that draws raves; blueberry, strawberry, or raspberry shortcake; and several different types of cookies, including Bob's renowned hermit cookies, a molasses-based confection chock-full of raisins.

Cindy's closes each night at around 7 p.m.; however, if you happen to roll in after that hour and Bob is still there, he'll happily relight his stove and heat up his fryers to make you a meal. Other places may be open later, but few are as accommodating as Cindy's when it comes to bending the rules for weary, hungry customers.

# Shaw's Fish & Lobster Wharf

129 Route 32, New Harbor, ME 04554 | (207) 677-2200 | Open mid-May to mid-October

The drive from U.S. 1 down to the small fishing village of New Harbor is a long one, but it's well worth it when you reach the scenic hamlet and especially when you sit yourself down at Shaw's for some authentically fresh, tasty, right-off-the-boat seafood.

One of Shaw's strengths is that it is part restaurant and part commercial fishing operation. This guarantees the freshest of fish, especially the lobster, which is unloaded on the dock several times a day and hustled into the restaurant's waiting coldwater tanks.

Another interesting feature at Shaw's is the Hardy Boat Cruises operation, which shares dock space with Shaw's. The Hardy boats depart twice daily for Monhegan Island, and they have special cruises for puffin and seal watches, lighthouse cruises, and fall coastal tours.

The cruise ship operation occupies most of the first floor of Shaw's, while the upper floor houses Shaw's restaurant. You can get up there via an outdoor staircase that puts you on a picnic-table-covered deck with a fetching panorama of the harbor and the nearby outlet to the sea. It's a great place to enjoy a meal or just to soak up the view.

## CHECK OUT THE RESTAURANT

This truly is a working harbor. As co-owner Lloyd Mendelson points out, you won't see a sailboat or cabin cruiser moored anywhere. This is good news for diners who crave seafood fresh off the boat. Lloyd has owned and managed Shaw's since 1990, and sometimes he feels married to the business. For years a cigar-puffing overseer who walked the decks of his establishment, he has been forced by state ordinance to take his smoking to his adjacent commercial dock, but he doesn't seem to mind. You'll still see him walking the grounds

**FRESH** lobsters being offloaded onto Shaw's dock.

day and night, making sure that customers are happy and things are running smoothly.

If you can pry yourself away from the magnificent view on the deck, proceed to the restaurant's interior, where there's a spacious pine-paneled, linoleum-floored dining room with sliding glass windows that admit welcome, sea-fresh breezes all day long. All the tables, indoors and out, have a nice assortment of condiments (including malt vinegar) on wooden trays and a spooled roll of paper towels in lieu of napkins. (That makes *me* feel right at home!)

At the rear of the room is the varnished-wood order counter staffed by half a dozen or more workers who are eager to take your request and speed it back to the fry cooks and other chefs in the kitchen. Chances are you won't have to wait long, even though all the food is made to order, so don't wander too far away.

## CHICKEN?!

The menu offerings at Shaw's are deep and varied. In addition to fried and broiled seafood dinners, there are steaks, salads, burgers, hot dogs—even a chicken Philly steak. Lloyd says that he sells a lot of chicken. Who to? Mostly locals, apparently. With all this great seafood from nearby waters on hand, they must surely be jaded diners who need a break from the bounty of the sea from time to time.

Boiled fresh lobster is very popular here, and you may have the single lobster, the double, or—drum roll—the triple! Lloyd says the double is the most popular, but triples are ordered quite frequently as well.

Another lobster dish that draws raves is the lobster pie, which consists of a thick lobster bisque poured into a pie crust, then covered with cracker crumbs and baked to a buttery crispness. Shore dinners of lobster and steamed clams move well in the summer months. Both dishes are served with drawn butter, salad or slaw, and a roll.

Chowders are of the Maine variety, with a light, creamy, buttery broth and generous chunks of seafood. You may choose between clam chowder, fish chowder with large chunks of firm pollock, Maine lobster stew, or the Maine seafood chowder, which is packed with clams, Maine shrimp, and scallops.

Speaking of Maine shrimp, Shaw's harvests its own during the winter months, and freezes them up to be served all summer long. The clams are also of local origin, coming from a supplier in nearby Waldoboro three times a week.

## A BUSY DEEP FRYER

The deep fryer serves up puffy, chewy whole-belly clams, as well as haddock, Maine shrimp, oysters, and scallops. The breading is a secret combination of ingredients that ensure a light, crispy crunch that doesn't get in the way of the flavorful seafood sealed inside. The french fries are definitely better than most of the ones you'll get at other shacks; they're thin cut and cooked firm and crisp.

Lobster rolls are big sellers, and with good reason. Shaw's picks its own lobster meat every day, and whatever isn't used gets the heave-ho. One last thing to keep in mind: Every day at 2 p.m. Shaw's raw bar opens on the first floor at the end of the dock, right next to the gift shop and tour boat operation. You can grab a dozen oysters or clams on the half shell, order a glass of beer or wine, and settle into one of several picnic tables at the end of the dock and watch the boats come and go in the harbor.

There's only one thing that's not good about Shaw's: having to go home!

## The Invention of the Fried Clam Strip

Back in the 1930s, Greek immigrant Thomas Soffron and his brothers settled in Ipswich, Massachusetts, the nexus of the burgeoning soft-shell clam industry, and they cast about for some sort of business to start up. Not a fan of the locally popular deep-fried, whole-belly clams, Soffron one day procured some larger hard-shell clams, sliced 1/8-inch-thick strips from the clam "feet" that protruded from the shells, fried them up, and found them to be delicious. Thus was the clam strip invented.

Several years later in the 1940s, Soffron made the acquaintance of Howard Johnson of roadside restaurant fame. He introduced Johnson to his clam strips, claiming that they had an advantage over whole-bellied clams because they tasted just as good, plus they kept longer and traveled better. Soffron thought they would make a nice addition to the Howard Johnson's menu. Johnson tried some and took immediately to the sweet, chewy flavor and texture of the clam strips. Soffron signed a deal with the restaurant chain to be their exclusive provider of strips, which were marketed under the name Tender-sweet Fried Clams.

Johnson rolled out Soffron's clam strips to his entire chain of restaurants, which was rapidly expanding from its New England roots into a nationwide operation. The quaint regional dish was an instant hit and grew in popularity along with Howard Johnson's restaurants and hotels. Americans everywhere soon became aware of fried clam strips and their tender, sweet flavor, and though the Howard Johnson's chain is no more, clam strips are still served today in seafood restaurants throughout the nation.

# Cod End

12 Commercial Street, Tenants Harbor, ME 04860 | (207) 372-6782 | www.codend.com
**Open mid-June to early September**

The first thing many customers ask when they walk through the front door of this rough-hewn-wood-planked cookhouse and seafood market is: "What's a cod end?" We'll get to that in a minute.

Cod End is a thirty-eight-year-old business founded, owned, and run by the Miller family, who moved up the rugged Maine coast from Cape Porpoise in southern Maine in the early 1970s. At that time, "Red" Miller decided to get more involved in the fishing and lobstering businesses, and he chose picturesque Tenants Harbor as a new home for his family. As the Millers settled into their new surroundings, Red's wife, Anne, thought it would be nice to serve some good local food from their dock on the harbor, so she started boiling lobsters and

**COD** End at low tide.

baking pies and serving them up to the tourists and locals. That's how Cod End came to be.

## REDOLENT OF MARITIME HISTORY

This place has all the authenticity and feel of a Down East fishing and lobstering operation from days gone by. Everything about Cod End is simple and understated, from the quaint chalkboard sign leaning against a bush out front announcing the day's specials to the wide-planked-wood fish market, cookhouse, deck, and pier that hang suspended over the harbor waters.

Anne Miller lovingly shaped Cod End's food operation for more than thirty years, doing much of the cooking and baking herself. She developed numerous recipes and specials, many of which still appear regularly on the menu. Anne and Red's daughter Susan, who grew up with the operation, has been running Cod End since 2007, and she has kept the shack's fine traditions and recipes alive and well.

Strawberry-blond, kinky-haired, and lightly freckled, Susan runs the cookhouse and fish market in a way that would make her mother proud. She's constantly on the move between the kitchen, the fish market counter, and her tiny office in the attic rafters above the market floor. During the off season when she's not involved with her work as a reflexologist, she goes out with her octogenarian father on his lobster boat and gives him a hand with his traps.

**COD** End's daily specials keep 'em coming back for more.

All great shacks have distinctive chowders and seafood stews, and Cod End is no exception. There's a fine fish chowder here and a meaty lobster stew. Then there's Anne Miller's tomato-based Mediterranean Seafood Stew, a particular favorite with regular customers. This dish is so tasty and so distinctive that it's a featured recipe in Brooke Dojny's excellent *New England Clam Shack Cookbook*. Chock-full of locally harvested clams, mussels, and fish, and lots of vegetables, a cup or bowl of this hearty and uplifting original stew will put you in good spirits for the rest of the day.

Cod End has three cooks working full time during the shack's relatively short season from mid-June to Labor Day. One cook handles the grill, while another tends to the always busy lobster pot. Fry cook Sue Dean has been at Cod End for nearly ten years, and she serves up copious quantities of fried clams, Maine shrimp, scallops, and haddock in the form of dinners, baskets, and side orders, all crispy, sweet, lightly breaded, and oh-so-fresh. Susan's niece, Stephanie Miller, who has been schooled in the culinary arts, is a constant presence in Cod End's busy cookhouse and part of the continuing Miller family Cod End tradition.

## FIERCELY LOCAL ABOUT SEAFOOD

All the seafood here is extremely local: the clams come from a local digger, lobsters are provided by Red and other area lobstermen, and the rest comes from nearby Port Clyde. Susan takes great pride in supporting the local fishing fleets. The Millers are, after all, part of the tightly knit maritime community in these parts. The fish the Millers purchase from Port Clyde are transported whole to Cod End's fish market, where they are cut fresh each day.

Other cookhouse dishes of note are the steamed clams and mussels, the shore dinner featuring steamed lobster, clams, mussels, and corn, and Cod End's famous homemade coleslaw, prepared daily. If you see something you like in the display cases in the fish market but you don't want to take it home and cook it up yourself, Susan and her staff will prepare it for you on the premises any way you wish.

## STILL BAKING AFTER ALL THESE YEARS

Pies are still baked fresh daily in the cookhouse. All the vegetables are from local sources, and the breads are from nearby Rockland. There are non-seafood choices such as burgers, salads, hot dogs, and other standard shack fare, such as grilled cheese sandwiches. Be sure to check out the daily specials—items whipped up in the kitchen based on whatever came off the boats that day. Susan says the specials are what keep the locals and the summer residents coming back regularly. They never know what they're going to get, and they're never disappointed.

So, what exactly *is* a cod end? "It's the belly of the fish net on an otter trawling rig, where all the fish end up after the net has dragged along the sea bottom," explains Susan. Picture a large, balloon-like fish net billowing underwater off the back of a commercial fishing boat and tapering down to a funnel-like tip. This "cod end" has a small opening at the rear that is large enough to allow water and smaller fish to escape but too small for grown fish to slip through. The cod end is where you'll find all those wonderful haddock, cod, other delectable North Atlantic fish that have made this part of the world famous.

So, if you're lucky enough to find yourself in the tiny fishing village of Tenants Harbor, Maine, in the summertime, allow yourself to be swept into the cod end of Cod End and enjoy a little slice of maritime Maine and the tasty local bounty from their little corner of the sea.

# Bagaduce Lunch

145 Frank Flat Road, Penobscot, ME 04476 | (207) 326-4197 | Open May to mid-September

**B**oy, is this place hard to find! If you've got GPS, be sure to lock in the coordinates for the address and pay close attention as you motor along. To get to this out-of-the-way shack, you'll travel down miles of country roads with only occasional glimpses of water here and there. Most of the scenery along the way consists of modest homes and small farm-type operations, with no hint that you're anywhere near the sea, except for the occasional stack of lobster traps outside a house or barn.

Just about where the tiny townships of North Brooksville, Penobscot, and Sedgwick meet and right next to a low-slung bridge over the Bagaduce River, you'll find an unassuming white-washed roadside stand with red trim. Nailed to its pitched roof is a simple hand-painted, black-and-white-lettered sign indicating that, yes, you've arrived at Bagaduce Lunch.

## THE AMAZING REVERSING FALLS

While you're scratching your head, wondering why on earth there's a clam shack in such a remote place, be sure to take in some of the local scenery—then perhaps you'll understand why. For starters, there's an unusual "reversing falls" beneath the bridge next to the shack. Actually, it isn't really a falls at all. Twice daily at low tide, water flows downstream beneath the bridge, sometimes at great speed, as it heads through a narrow gap toward its ocean outlet a dozen or so miles away. It flows the opposite way with equal force several hours later when the tide surges back in. The bridge by Bagaduce traverses a narrow channel cut between rocky banks that gives the spot its falls-like appearance of rushing waters.

Whitewater kayakers love the thrill of riding

**BAGADUCE** Lunch was rebuilt from the ground up in 2010.

the swift current, and you may see them shooting the rapids while you're there. Daring swimmers sometimes jump in and take the quick, joyous trip under the bridge, also. If such is your inclination, you do so at your own risk, and a life vest is certainly recommended if you decide to take the plunge.

Upriver from the falls and just beyond Bagaduce's picturesque picnic-tabled backyard is a pond-like swell in the river with a lovely tree-covered islet in the middle. This idyllic scene is your backdrop while feasting on lunch (or dinner) at Bagduce.

## NEW DIGS

As for the shack itself, Bagaduce (pronounced bag-uh-DOOS) Lunch was completely rebuilt from the ground up just in time for the 2010 season. Co-owners Judy Astbury and her husband Mike are thrilled with the new quarters (though from the outside it looks a lot like the old place, only much newer and a bit bigger). Judy is particularly happy with the expanded kitchen area, where all their delectables are prepared and cooked to order. She usually works the counter, while Mike mans the fryers. It's pretty much a family affair through and through, with the Astburys' daughters, one of Judy's cousins, and a niece helping out behind the counter and in the kitchen during the busy times.

## Gifford's Ice Cream: The Pride of Maine

The vast majority of clam shacks in New England serve ice cream of one sort or another, and many of the finer shacks sell a regionally famous brand that comes from the town of Skowhegan in the agricultural heart of central Maine.

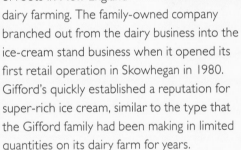

Gifford's Ice Cream prides itself on its small-town values and its five generations of roots in New England dairy farming. The family-owned company branched out from the dairy business into the ice-cream stand business when it opened its first retail operation in Skowhegan in 1980. Gifford's quickly established a reputation for super-rich ice cream, similar to the type that the Gifford family had been making in limited quantities on its dairy farm for years.

Shortly thereafter, they began supplying other ice-cream stands and small eateries, initially in Maine and eventually throughout New England. Gifford's makes about forty different flavors of ice cream, including Apple Pie, Maine Wild Blueberry, Maine Lobster Tracks, and Chocolate Rainforest Crunch.

Numerous clam shacks proudly offer Gifford's fine, premium ice creams on their dessert menus. If you pull up to a shack and see the Gifford's sign displayed, you'll know you're in for a treat.

The menu at Bagaduce, like the location, is deceptively plain, featuring local seafood and a variety of grilled sandwiches, fresh homemade slaws and salads (be sure to try the three-bean), and a variety of home-baked pies for dessert. Judy's brother is a lobsterman, and he brings his fresh catch to Bagaduce daily. And all the haddock, scallops, clams, and Maine shrimp are locally sourced from Maine suppliers. The Astburys are rightfully proud of supporting the local fishermen and farmers whenever they stock their kitchen.

## FOUR GENERATIONS AND COUNTING

This unusual eatery dates back to the 1940s, when it was originally opened by Judy's grandparents, who ran Bagaduce Lunch in their own quiet, modest way for the next thirty years. Judy began working at Bagaduce when she was just ten years old, and she has stuck with the family business ever since. Her parents were also involved, but when it came time for succession in 1997, Judy and Mike stepped

**A** vintage postcard showing the original Bagaduce Lunch.

forward and took the reins.

The Astburys have kept the same family recipes at the core of the menu through the years: a simple offering of deep-fried seafood baskets, rolls, burgers, hot dogs, salads and slaws, homemade pies, and Gifford's Ice Cream, a Maine favorite.

## JAMES BEARD APPROVES

You may be tempted to write this place off as a quaint yet remote curiosity, perhaps not worth the extra mileage and navigational effort it takes to get here. However, before you do, consider this: Bagaduce's won the coveted James Beard Foundation America's Classics award in 2008 as a unique and distinctive American eatery. Judy has the plaque behind the counter to prove it. There aren't many (if any) other clam shacks that can claim any sort of distinction like this. It's a testament to the true originality, honesty, integrity (and worthiness!) of Bagaduce Lunch. What are you waiting for? Switch on that GPS, hit the road, and check this place out!

# Jordan's Snack Bar

**200 Downeast Highway, Ellsworth, ME 04605 | (207) 667-2174 | Open early March to early November**

There are two routes out of Ellsworth, Maine, that take travelers to nearby attractions: One goes south to the busy town of Bar Harbor and neighboring Acadia National Park, which boasts perhaps the nicest stretch of rocky coastline on the Eastern Seaboard. The other route, known as the Downeast Highway (U.S. Route 1), heads east out of town toward the Canadian border and passes through lovely, unspoiled Maine seacoast towns that offer a pleasant contrast to the often more tourist-packed cities and towns further south along Maine's coastline.

If you choose to go the Downeast route (or if you simply need a clam fix before heading to Bar Harbor and Acadia), be sure to stop in at Jordan's Snack Bar on the Downeast Highway a mile or so east of downtown Ellsworth.

This quaint, clean, unassuming shack at first appears to be primarily an ice-cream and burger stand (there's a large ice-cream cone sign atop the building). But there's more to this place . . . *so* much more.

For starters, Jordan's has three order windows and one pickup window on the front of

**JORDAN'S** Snack Bar on an unusually quiet day.

the building, which should be your first tipoff that this is indeed a very busy place when it gets humming. Country music twangs away through outdoor speakers. Once you've made your way to the front of the line and placed your order, hang tight or take a seat at one of the picnic tables in front of Jordan's right next to busy Route 1. When you've snagged your order, then you're ready to explore all that Jordan's Snack Bar has to offer.

## COUNTRY MUSIC AND HOT RODS

Some people retire to their cars in the parking lot, pop open their Styrofoam containers, and

**JORDAN'S** hard-working kitchen crew.

dig into their feasts, drive-in style. Those who prefer to dine alfresco will find a cool, shaded picnic area on the west side of the shack. There are numerous picnic tables, a nicely designed playground for kids, and whimsical painted statues of bear cubs shinnying high up on the trunks of several trees in the grove.

If you prefer to escape the elements and dine indoors, there's a spacious building just to the east of Jordan's that's filled with some twenty formica-topped tables. The dining hall is air-conditioned, making it a welcome sanctuary on hot, muggy days.

There's still more to this place. To the east of the dining hall is an open-air building where, every Wednesday night in the summer, a country and western band plays for free. Half the pavilion is set aside for line dancing (a popular local activity), and the other half is for the band and audience. Just to the east of the music hall is a massive parking lot where car rallies are also held on Wednesday nights. Auto enthusiasts come from miles around to show off their wheels and to gawk at everyone else's.

Music and dancing and souped-up cars not your thing? In back of the music pavilion, there's a games arcade in a large converted garage space that's filled with pinball and computer games and a couple of pool tables. Between the picnic area playground and the arcade building, youngsters will find plenty of distractions while the family dines on Jordan's fine seafood, sandwiches, and ice cream.

## FROM HUMBLE BEGINNINGS

Founder James (Jimmy) Jordan dreamed up this miniature theme park of food and entertainment in eastern Maine some thirty years ago. Jimmy and his forbears were blueberry rakers and tree farmers, common occupations for native Mainers at the time. Starting with just the food shack in 1981, Jimmy got his wife and kids involved with helping out in the kitchen and at the order windows. As business picked up, he started buying adjacent properties, transforming each one into a new part of his budding entertainment empire. More than fifteen additions have been made to the business over the years, most in the first several years of operation, as Jordan's Snack Bar took off and quickly became a magnet for locals and for tourists passing through Ellsworth on busy Route 1.

Jimmy passed away in spring 2010, leaving Jordan's in the capable hands of his son Shawn, who has been involved in the business almost from the beginning. Shawn says he was raised in Jordan's kitchen, and he exerts the same level of energy and enthusiasm that his father brought to the business for nearly thirty years.

The Jordan's complex now covers several acres, much of it focused on family dining and entertainment. As Shawn says, "You win over the kids, and you win over the parents." That's been the key to Jordan's long-standing success.

## KEEPING IT SIMPLE— AND QUICK

Although Jordan's has grown and diversified over the years, the kitchen operation and the menu have remained simple and streamlined in order to get high quality food to customers as quickly as possible. Shawn is obsessive about efficiency in the kitchen, and he boasts that everything they serve at Jordan's takes no longer than four minutes to prepare and four minutes to cook. This guarantees hot, fresh food that keeps the line of customers moving quickly.

The menu focuses on deep-fried seafood and grilled sandwiches, and that seems to be fine with the mostly local clientele. Jordan's top seller is the fried clams, small and crisp and procured from Ipswich Seafood, the biggest and most reliable supplier of fresh clams in New England.

The fried scallops here are large, firm, chewy, and full of flavor. The fried haddock fillets are also particularly fresh and flaky and of local origin. If you need to choose between french fries and onion rings for your side dish, go with the rings. They're hand-cut in the kitchen throughout the day, and each serving is made to order, as are all the seafood platters and virtually everything else on the menu.

Jordan's offers Maine-based Gifford's ice cream. Be sure to save room for a cup or a cone. This is Maine's finest frozen treat and a great way to cap off a meal of deep-fried delights.

Though Jordan's may be a destination spot mostly for locals, anyone with a taste for fine fried seafood, perfectly grilled burgers, or cool refreshing ice cream should definitely seek this place out when exploring or passing through this beautiful part of Maine. And if you happen to love both country music and fried clams, then this place is very likely your little slice of heaven.

**JT's SEAFOOD**

**Ted's FRIED CLAMS**
Since 1950
**ROCK HOUSE ICE CREAM**

LUNCH SPECIAL
8OZ BURGER
FRIES SODA 699
THURSDAYS
ICE CREAM DAY

OPEN Thursday thru Sunday
11am to 9pm

FRIENDLY FISHERMA
FISH MARK
FISH & CHI
FRIED CLA
FRUIT & PROD

**Tony's CLAM SHOPPE**

**SHAWS FISH & LOBSTE WHARF**

LOBSTER SHACK RESTAURANT

**Bob's CLAM HUT**

**OPEN Year Round**

ESSEX SEAFOOD
RESTAURANT & FISH MARKET
OPEN YEAR ROUND
LOBSTER

WOODMAN'S
OF ESSEX
SINCE 1914

FRESH LOBSTER
THE
BEST
AROUND
CRAB ROLLS

Cindy's CHOWDER HOUSE

CLAM BOX

THE ICE HOUSE

KEN'S PLACE

FAMOUS FOR
SEAFOODS
SINCE 1927

★ WELCOME
★ FRESH SEAFOOD
CHILDRENS MENU

KEN'S
Raw Bar

OPEN

FISH
LOBSTER
CLAMS

# Canadian Clam Shacks

Although our neighbors to the north don't refer to them as "clam shacks," Canada's maritime provinces do have some excellent, casual, dine-in-the-rough seafood eateries that are well worth checking out if you happen to be up that way. Keep in mind that many of the clams and much of the haddock and cod served in New England clam shacks is harvested in Canadian waters, so you're pretty much guaranteed some great, fresh seafood at these establishments. Here are some suggestions for the provinces of New Brunswick and Nova Scotia:

## New Brunswick

Ossie's Lunch
125 Glebe Road
Chamcook, NB
(506) 755-2758

Chez Leo Fried Clams
3868 Route 134 Highway
Shediac, NB
(506) 532-4543

Fred's
2470 Chemin Acadie
Cap-Pele, NB

Cantine de la Plage
612 Rue Acadie
Grande Anse, NB

Sheila Dairy Bar
Tracadie-Sheila, NB

King Street Takeout
St. Stephen, NB

Cave View Family Restaurant
82 Bay View Road
St. Martin's, NB

## Nova Scotia

Chez l'Ami
1730 Highway 1
Church Point, NS
(902) 769-0001

Chez Jean
3139 Highway 1
Belliveau Cove, NS
(902) 837-5750

Ed's Take-Out
Highway 303
Digby, NS
(902) 245-2071

Harbour Fish N' Fries
7886 Highway 7
Musquodoboit Harbour, NS
(902) 889-3366

Seaside Seafoods
6943 Highway 3
Hunts Point, NS
(902) 683-2618

# Clam Shacks by Type

If you're looking for a certain type of clam shack—for instance, one that caters to families, one that parties hearty, one that has great views or unusual food, or whatever—the following lists should be helpful in narrowing the field of shacks down to those that may be of most interest to you.

## FAMILY SHACKS

*Clam shacks are by nature family places, but these stand out as particularly family-friendly.*

Lenny and Joe's Fish Tale, Madison, CT
Iggy's Doughboys, Warwick, RI
Arnold's Lobster & Clam Bar, Eastham, MA
Woodman's, Essex, MA
Bob's Clam Hut, Kittery, ME
Ken's Place, Scarborough, ME
Jordan's Snack Bar, Ellsworth, ME

## FUNKY SHACKS

*These shacks exude a more offbeat look and atmosphere.*

Stowe's Seafood, West Haven, CT
The Place, Guilford, CT
The Clam Castle, Madison, CT
Johnny Ad's Drive-In, Old Saybrook, CT
Flo's Clam Shack, Middletown and Portsmouth, RI
Friendly Fisherman, North Eastham, MA
Essex Seafood, Essex, CT
The Clam Shack, Kennebunkport, ME
Benny's Famous Fried Clams, Portland, ME
Cindy's Fish & Chips, Freeport, ME

## ROMANTIC SHACKS

*You may not want to pop the question at a clam shack, but the following are nice spots for a tête-à-tête with someone special.*

The Place, Guilford, CT
Hallmark Drive-In, Old Lyme, CT
Evelyn's Drive-In, Tiverton, RI
Cobie's Clam Shack, Brewster, MA
JT's Seafood, Brewster, MA
J. T. Farnham's, Essex, MA
The Lobster Shack at Two Lights, Cape Elizabeth, ME
Cod End, Tenants Harbor, ME

## PARTY SHACKS

*These shacks tend to get down a little more and exude a more party-like atmosphere.*

The Place, Guilford, CT
Flo's Clam Shack, Middletown, RI
Woodman's, Essex, MA

## SHACKS WITH A VIEW

*Whether it's the beach, a harbor, the ocean, a marsh, or a pretty stretch of road, these shacks boast nice scenery to gaze upon while you dine.*

Chick's Drive-In, West Haven, CT
Hallmark Drive-In, Old Lyme, CT
Costello's Clam Shack, Noank, CT
Sea View, Mystic, CT
Johnny Angel's Clam Shack, Charlestown, RI
Champlin's Seafood Deck, Galilee, RI
Monahan's Clam Shack by the Sea, Narragansett, RI

Iggy's Doughboys, Warwick, RI
Blount Clam Shack, Warren, RI
Flo's Clam Shack, Middletown, RI
Evelyn's Drive-In, Tiverton, RI
The Clam Shack, Falmouth, MA
Tony's Clam Shop, Quincy, MA
J. T. Farnham's, Essex, MA
Markey's Lobster Pool, Seabrook, NH
Brown's Lobster Pound, Seabrook, NH
The Lobster Shack at Two Lights, Cape Elizabeth, ME
Harraseeket Lunch, South Freeport, ME
Shaw's Fish, New Harbor, ME
Cod End, Tenants Harbor, ME
Bagaduce Lunch, Penobscot, ME

## CITY SHACKS

*These shacks have a more urban feel to them, given their locations in or near major population centers.*
Stowe's Seafood, West Haven, CT
Chick's Drive-In, West Haven, CT
Fred's Shanty, New London, CT
Iggy's Doughboys, Warwick, RI
Tony's Clam Shop, Quincy, MA
Benny's Famous Fried Clams, Portland, ME

## SHACKS WITH UNUSUAL MENUS

*If you're looking for more exotic dishes than you'll find at many clam shacks, these shacks are good bets for something out of the ordinary.*
The Place, Guilford, CT

Cove Clam Shack, Mystic, CT
Aunt Carrie's, Narragansett, RI
Evelyn's Drive-In, Tiverton, RI
Tony's Clam Shop, Quincy, MA
Cindy's Fish & Chips, Freeport, ME
Cod End, Tenants Harbor, ME

## LAID-BACK SHACKS

*These shacks offer a slower pace and a more contemplative atmosphere.*
Stowe's Seafood, West Haven, CT
The Place, Guilford, CT
Johnny Angel's Clam Shack, Charlestown, RI
Evelyn's Drive-In, Tiverton, RI
Friendly Fisherman, North Eastham, MA
Captain Frosty's, Dennis, MA
J. T. Farnham's, Essex, MA
The Ice House, Rye, NH
Benny's Famous Fried Clams, Portland, ME
Calder's Clam Shack, Chebeague Island, ME
Bagaduce Lunch, Penobscot, ME

## SHACKS WITH GREAT INTERIORS

*If your eyes demand entertainment while you dine indoors, these shacks have interiors that feature unique, often outrageous, décor and/or a nice indoor dining atmosphere.*
Stowe's Seafood, West Haven, CT
The Clam Castle, Madison, CT
Aunt Carrie's, Narragansett, RI
Starboard Galley, Narragansett, RI
Flo's Clam Shack, Middletown, RI
Evelyn's Drive-In, Tiverton, RI

Cooke's Seafood, Mashpee, MA
Kream 'n' Kone, West Dennis, MA
JT's Seafood, Brewster, MA
J. T. Farnham's, Essex, MA
Woodman's, Essex, MA
Brown's Lobster Pound, Seabrook, NH
The Ice House, Rye, NH
Bob's Clam Hut, Kittery, ME
Cod End, Tenants Harbor, ME

## SHACKS WITH GREAT EXTERIORS

*Part of the fun of going to a clam shack is beholding the funky, weather-beaten, or retro look of the place from the outside. Check out these contenders.*

The Clam Castle, Madison, CT
Johnny Ad's Drive-In, Old Saybrook, CT
Sea View, Mystic, CT
Sea Swirl, Mystic, CT
Aunt Carrie's, Narragansett, RI
Iggy's Doughboys, Warwick, RI
Blount Clam Shack, Warren, RI
Flo's Clam Shack, Middletown, RI
The Clam Shack, Falmouth, MA
Arnold's Lobster & Clam Bar, Eastham, MA
Cobie's Clam Shack, Brewster, MA
JT's Seafood, Brewster, MA
Captain Frosty's, Dennis, MA
The Clam Box, Ipswich, MA
The Clam Shack, Kennebunkport, ME
Benny's Famous Fried Clams, Portland, ME
Cindy's Fish & Chips, Freeport, ME
Cod End, Tenants Harbor, ME

Bagaduce Lunch, Penobscot, ME

## SHACKS WITH GREAT OUTDOOR DINING

*Dining in the rough is a big part of the clam shack experience. These shacks offer great alfresco dining.*

Chick's Drive-In, West Haven, CT
The Place, Guilford, CT
Lenny and Joe's Fishtale, Madison, CT
Hallmark Drive-In, Old Lyme, CT
Costello's Clam Shack, Noank, CT
Sea View, Mystic, CT
Johnny Angel's Clam Shack, Charlestown, RI
Blount Clam Shack, Warren, RI
Evelyn's Drive-In, Tiverton, RI
The Clam Shack, Falmouth, MA
Kream 'n' Kone, West Dennis, MA
Arnold's Lobster & Clam Bar, Eastham, MA
Friendly Fisherman, North Eastham, MA
Captain Frosty's, Dennis, MA
The Clam Box, Ipswich, MA
The Ice House, Rye, NH
The Lobster Shack at Two Lights, Cape Elizabeth, ME
Benny's Famous Fried Clams, Portland, ME
Harraseeket Lunch, South Freeport, ME
Shaw's Fish, New Harbor, ME
Cod End, Tenants Harbor, ME
Bagaduce Lunch, Penobscot, ME
Jordan's Snack Bar, Ellsworth, ME

# Index

# Photo Credits

# Acknowledgments

There are a number of people who have been of great assistance in my research and writing of this guidebook, and I hereby acknowledge them as follows:

The clam shack owners and managers, who graciously and patiently took me into their establishments, showed me around, shared their stories, answered my questions, and assisted in any way they could to help me get as clear a picture as possible of what makes each of their shacks unique, appealing, and worth a special visit.

John Whalen, publisher of Cider Mill Press, a colleague and friend for many years who agreed to publish this guide as part of his fine line of books.

Fred Liebling, a close friend since childhood, who graciously allowed me to stay with him on several occasions at his seaside house in Maine while I conducted my research up and down the Maine coast through the spring, summer, and fall.

Pippa Jack of *Rhode Island Monthly* magazine and my friend Charles Hayes, both of whom made good recommendations for clam shacks in and around Narragansett Bay and Rhode Island.

Jim Henry, Cape Cod native and personal friend in our hometown of Old Saybrook, Connecticut, who made numerous fine suggestions of Cape shacks to explore and include. Jim's sense of what makes a good lobster roll is unmatched.

My wife, Ellen, and our four children—Nicholas, Natalie, Brian, and Max—who waited patiently at home while I spent days (and nights) on the road doing research. Their sweet reward was often a copious bag of leftover shack fare that I'd bring home for their consumption. (Thanks also for keeping the noise level down during the writing process.)

Vicky Vaughn Shea, my frequent partner on book projects, who designed and laid out the book with her usual creativity, professionalism, optimism, and good cheer. Here's hoping we continue to work on many projects together in the future.

Jessie Shiers, editor, whom I admire greatly for her editorial skills, her intelligence, and her swiftness in helping to bring this project (and many others we've worked on together) to fruition.

If I've forgotten anyone, please forgive me. Though I seem to have kept my body weight in check throughout the research phase of the project, I have no idea what my cholesterol count may be these days; if high cholesterol from an overdose of wonderful, deep-fried seafood has had an adverse effect on my memory, I wouldn't be the least bit surprised.

*Bon appétit!*

# About the Author

**MIKE URBAN** is an editor, writer, and book packager who specializes in travel, outdoor recreation, sports, and business/career books. He has been in book publishing for more than thirty years, working for such companies as Rand McNally, World Book, NTC Publishing Group, and the Globe Pequot Press. Mike served as vice president and associate publisher of Globe Pequot for more than ten years, where he edited hundreds of travel guides and created such guidebook series as *Fun with the Family*, *Discover Historic America*, *Quick Escapes*, *Curiosities*, *Winter Trails*, and the *Cheap Bastard's Guides*. He lives in Old Saybrook, Connecticut.

*(If you have comments or suggestions about the material in this guidebook, you're welcome to share them with the author by e-mailing him at mikeurban615@gmail.com.)*

## About Cider Mill Press Book Publishers

**GOOD IDEAS RIPEN WITH TIME.** From seed to harvest, Cider Mill Press strives to bring fine reading, information, and entertainment together between the covers of its creatively crafted books. Our Cider Mill bears fruit twice a year, publishing a new crop of titles each spring and fall.

Visit us on the web at
www.cidermillpress.com
or write to us at
12 Port Farm Road
Kennebunkport, Maine 04046